Dylan's Endeavour

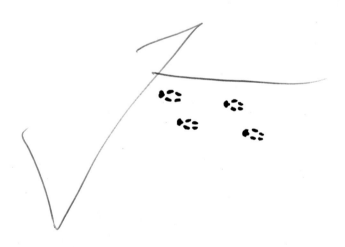

John Roe

With what seemed like an unearthly tearing sound, the screen gave way and Dylan found himself sailing through the opening in a shower of broken glass. (page 65)

Illustrations by

Peter Roe

NEVADA HOUSE PUBLISHING
&
TRAFFORD PUBLISHING

For Karen

This story has been a long time coming...

Text & illustrations copyright © John Roe 2002

Published by **NEVADA HOUSE PUBLISHING**
in collaboration with **TRAFFORD PUBLISHING**
Printed in Victoria, Canada

National Library of Canada Cataloguing in Publication

Roe, John, 1942-
 Dylan's endeavour / John Roe ; illustrated by Peter Roe.
Includes bibliographical references and index.
ISBN 1-55369-758-8
 1. Dogs--Anecdotes. I. Title.
SF426.2.R63 2002   C813'.6   C2002-903346-2

TRAFFORD

This book was published *on-demand* in cooperation with Trafford Publishing.
On-demand publishing is a unique process and service of making a book available for retail sale to the public taking advantage of on-demand manufacturing and Internet marketing.
On-demand publishing includes promotions, retail sales, manufacturing, order fulfilment, accounting and collecting royalties on behalf of the author.

Suite 6E, 2333 Government St., Victoria, B.C. V8T 4P4, CANADA
Phone   250-383-6864   Toll-free   1-888-232-4444 (Canada & US)
Fax   250-383-6804   E-mail   sales@trafford.com
Web site   www.trafford.com   TRAFFORD PUBLISHING IS A DIVISION OF TRAFFORD HOLDINGS LTD.
Trafford Catalogue #02-0571   www.trafford.com/robots/02-0571.html

10   9   8   7   6   5   4   3   2

Endeavour: *n.* a serious determined effort
Webster's New Collegiate Dictionary

Acknowledgements

First, to the two Peters in my family: my brother Peter who had the temerity to not only take me up on my request to provide honest criticisms but gave me sound suggestions to substantially improve the original manuscript and provided invaluable assistance throughout its gestation; my son Peter, a professional animator, who took up the challenge to provide illustrations that I feel greatly enhance the story. My debt to both is immense.

Secondly, to Gloria McDowell, editor emeritus, who made short work of any dangling participles and urged me not to delay any longer and offer it to an unsuspecting public.

Finally, last but not least Delia Dobson and Lianne Hill, who, not only suffered through three weeks of worry and constant searching, but were kind enough to take time with me to relive their harrowing experiences.

Author's Notes

This is the story of Dylan's Endeavour -- how a shy, young Welsh Springer Spaniel went missing in downtown Toronto and was found by me, his owner, nearly six weeks later in Oakville, only seven miles away from his home in Mississauga. From time immemorial there have been stories of remarkable exploits by animals, including journeys of much longer distances. What makes Dylan's story unique, however, are the circumstances.

The Toronto Star, which reported his return just before Christmas 1995, described it as an odyssey -- an incredible journey since, unfamiliar with big city life, he had had to negotiate some of the busiest traffic in Canada, including crossing several major multi-lane highways and three rivers. He also had to contend with some of the harshest early winter weather conditions experienced in decades, scavenge for food and, judging by his wounds and local newspaper reports at that time of such skirmishes, likely had to defend himself against coyotes. Yet, remarkably, when Dylan and I were reunited in an amazing real-life storybook ending, his battle scars were for the most part healing, and although he had lost a lot of weight, his mild temperament was generally unchanged.

This little chronicle is therefore dedicated to all those who truly understand, having experienced firsthand, that unique bond of love and empathy which can exist between humans and canines. It is a story that has had many a verbal recounting and I still shiver with each re-telling when I come to the part about our reunion; yes, it actually **did** happen that way.

As the reader will appreciate, I have taken license in describing Dylan's encounters, his actions, and feelings while on the run. These conjectures are the result of some sleuthing on my part: the nature and state of his various wounds when found; the weather conditions during those forty days; subsequent exploration of the terrain and knowledge of its wild inhabitants; reports from those who contacted me after his story appeared in *The Toronto Star* to tell me of their sightings; and last, but not least, the subtle changes in his behaviour.

All the *human* events are, however, true and the people and animals real. No liberties have been taken in changing names, places or even time frames to achieve dramatic effect. If there are errors of fact or misinterpretation of others' actions, motives or feelings, then these are solely mine. I do not know where to begin to acknowledge fully the debt my wife Karen and I owe to all those who were drawn into the search, who felt for and suffered with us and, when all seemed lost, were able to join in our profound rejoicing at Dylan's return. Delia, one of the key players in this tale, was vacationing in Bermuda when she got word of its happy ending. Calling long distance she exclaimed: "Is it REALLY true that you've found Dylan? We've got to write a story about this!"

Several years have passed since Dylan's adventure yet the events remain as fresh in my mind now as they were then. It is time to publish that story which, hopefully, will strike a kindred note in you, the reader.

JR
December 2002

Prologue

The two animals stared intently at each other. Dylan felt the hackles on his neck rise. In the weeks that he had been at large, he had never experienced such instant fear. There was something about the other dog – if that's what he was – that instantly identified him as an adversary. The other creature never flinched. Instead, eyes fixed on the apprehensive canine, he slowly began to come closer.

The pale winter sunlight had already begun to fade. The darkening shadows added to the menace of the moment. Even the sounds of distant traffic on the nearby multi-lane highway seemed to have been stilled. The only noise was the faintest crackle of dry leaves being trampled as the small German Shepherd/wolf-like dog continued to draw near.

All Dylan's senses were now on high alert. He had shed the numbing tiredness that had become so much a part of his days on the run. Now the Welsh Springer Spaniel could feel his body quivering with a tenseness alien to his timid nature. His once gleaming red and creamy white coat had become shaggy and unkempt through lack of daily grooming and the silky hair on his ears and long leg feathers was matted with burrs. To a casual observer chancing on this scene, it would have seemed that this was a confrontation between two wild dogs rather than a wild dog and a family pet.

For something had changed. The chemistry of fear, the smell of which predatory animals can always detect, had been replaced by a mounting fury of will that would have astonished those who knew him. Though not exactly a wimp, Dylan had always been shy and withdrawn, particularly when first meeting people and strange dogs. The other animal must have sensed the change for it hesitated and began to emit a curious, high pitched yipping sound. It was at that instant that Dylan knew that he was not dealing with another dog. Indeed, the other animal was a coyote, what North American Indians call one of "the ghosts of the forest".

Combining the sleekness of a cat, the quick intelligence of a fox, and the brute wildness of a wolf, the coyote is considered by naturalists to be the most numerous and successful large predator on the North American continent. Omnivorous, eating whatever is available, it will not infrequently prey on domestic animals such as cats and small dogs. Whereas wild cats and other carnivores depend on a combination of claws and teeth for killing their prey, a coyote relies on sharp enamel-capped teeth alone to immobilize and kill its quarry. Death occurs when its victim is grasped by the throat and suffocated. A coyote kill can always be identified by tooth punctures around the throat.

Dylan, naturally, knew nothing of this, but all his instincts told him he was in mortal danger.

Chapter 1

A dreadful shock

The direct flight from Capetown to Miami had been uneventful. As usual, Karen had managed to sleep most of the way. Now totally refreshed, she strode purposefully ahead of her husband as they switched terminals in preparation for the last leg of their long journey home to Mississauga near Toronto. They knew they had plenty of time to spare between flights so

Karen, always the planner, had decided to call her daughter Lianne from the airport once they made their connections. As far as John was concerned, news of what had been happening on the home front could wait until they actually touched down in Toronto. Then would be time enough to catch up on events and, more importantly, reassemble their household. Home would not be complete until they had collected Dylan and Fiona.

Dylan was their much-loved Welsh Springer Spaniel, the veritable apple of their eye, from the very first moment he had moved in with them two years previously. Their feelings for Fiona were less generous. Over the years this former barnyard cat had proven to be a real pest whenever they went away. Family and friends refused to look after her when she developed the bad habit of leaving anal and urinary "trophies". In recent years it had therefore become John and Karen's practice to put her into kennels. But, despite her nature, she too was family so they felt things would not be normal until they were reunited with both animals.

When they had left on their month-long vacation to South Africa, Lianne, already the mother of an eighteen-month-old, was seven months pregnant. Lianne had always been one to keep fit and there had been no complications with Lexi. Mothers being mothers, however, they worry, and Karen was no exception. She was also curious to know what was happening on their housing front. Just before John and Karen went away, Lianne's husband Paul had accepted a new high tech position in Ottawa so this meant putting their house in

Toronto up for sale and for Lianne, an elementary school teacher, it also meant winding up her job. It was little wonder, therefore, that at the last minute Lianne had balked at having Dylan stay with them as in the past. Instead, a quick change of plans resulted in Dylan being left with Delia, one of Karen's sisters, who also lived in Toronto, close to its downtown core.

Karen had decided that she would wait until 7:30 a.m. to call Lianne. As the appointed time arrived, John took charge of their hand luggage having been enjoined, as always, "Don't let anything out of your sight." It did not stop him, however, keeping a close eye on her as she engaged in conversation. Although too far away to hear anything, it quickly became clear that she was becoming increasingly distressed. John's mind started to race. He began to worry that perhaps something had gone wrong with Lianne's pregnancy. Finally Karen hung up the receiver and made her way back to him, her whole being a picture of misery.

"What's up?" John asked, already dreading her response. "It's Dylan", she replied in a hollow voice. "He's been missing for three weeks". Relieved that nothing was the matter with Lianne or other family members, John heard the words but their full import didn't sink in. Then he stammered: "Dylan? Missing? Three weeks? What happened?"

The story was starkly simple. It appeared that Dylan had been left with a dog sitter while Delia had gone away for the weekend taking her own two dogs with her. The dog sitter had taken Dylan to a nearby park where

Delia regularly exercised her dogs.   Once at the park, without really giving it a second thought, the sitter had unleashed him, at which point Dylan had taken off.   That, apart from an initial flood of reported sightings, was the last anyone had seen of him despite an extensive search, posted notices and regular contacts with all the Humane Societies in the Greater Toronto area.

Dylan missing... for three weeks... and in, of all places, Toronto, a metropolitan expanse with upwards of four million people stretching some thirty miles around the south western shore of Lake Ontario.   John could hardly take it in.   He stood there, his face as crumpled as he felt, a mixture of shock and anguish.   A multitude of thoughts immediately flooded his mind.   Dylan was an extremely shy dog by nature.   Although they lived in a large city, the west-end of Mississauga with its single family dwellings and tree-lined streets was a far cry from the big city bustle of Canada's largest metropolis. How could Dylan possibly survive?   It would be bad enough for a family pet to go missing in its neighbour-hood, but Toronto?   Day and night its downtown streets stream with cars, trucks, and electric streetcars. During the day cyclists add to the confusion as they weave their way in and out of the traffic as it moves constantly through the busy downtown.   To those used to its dissonant sights, sounds and smells, there is a comfortable familiarity.   It is the very essence of all that comprises a big city.   For those not used to big city life, particularly a timid dog, it would surely be a stressful, scary experience.   Poor Dylan!   How could he possibly be expected to cope on his own in that kind of environment?

To anyone who had seen Karen and John at Miami airport it must have been obvious that they were in total shock. Staring numbly at each other, the middle-aged couple was a picture of sheer despair and dejection. In a flash, all their good feelings about their month in South Africa dissipated. Was it really only yesterday that Karen, while gazing up at Table Mountain towering behind them as they enjoyed a final sun-soaked lunch on the waterfront, had exclaimed: "I've never felt more happy". Recalling that magic moment, she looked bleakly at John and said resignedly: "Is all happiness transitory?"

The two-hour flight between Miami and Toronto had to be the most difficult in their lives. Sunk in their individual miseries, each tried to cope in their very different ways with the reality of returning to a home without Dylan. As part of their travelling library, they had packed a currently popular book, *Men are from Mars, Women are from Venus*, which graphically described the differences in communication between men and women. Consistent with the author's premise, Karen couldn't stop talking, never seeming to draw a breath between seemingly disparate thoughts. "John, what are we going to do? You don't think he's still out there, do you? What if someone has taken him..." John, true to his "leave-me-alone-for-the-moment" male instincts, had retreated to his "cave", that inner sanctum where he could think things through, try to make sense of the situation, and to reflect...to other places and other times.

John had always loved dogs - not all dogs, of course. He had always thought he would like to have a Lassie-type dog, in particular a Border Collie. Apart from what he considered to be their handsome mien, they were clearly intelligent dogs as befit their stature as working dogs. Undoubtedly, his love for this breed was nourished by his childhood reading. Enid Blyton's *Shadow the Sheepdog* was a particular favourite and the fact that his namesake in the book had such a dog, one that was his constant companion and loyal to a fault, clearly left an indelible mark on an impressionable mind.

John thought he must have been about six or seven years old when his parents first got a dog, a black and white puppy of dubious origin. It was extremely messy, excessively noisy and impossibly chewy. In short, the little creature had nothing in his personality to endear himself to John's mother, never really a pet lover. As a result his stay in their household was short. John's parents soon got tired of him and gave him away. That was the last John saw of him. Sitting on the plane between Miami and Toronto, John was somewhat ashamed to realise that he could not remember the young pup's name.

But it had been a different story with **his** first dog. He recognised that his desire to have a dog of his own must have been a burden for his parents, struggling like so many others to bring up young families in post-World War II England. After experiencing active combat for some six years, his father had returned to small town banking in Sheringham, a summer seaside resort in North Norfolk. He must have found it some-what mundane after his war-time postings overseas to Africa and India. The house that John's parents bought after his father was de-mobbed required major renovations and ongoing expenditures so money was always tight.

As with so many of those who volunteered to go to war, John's father had experienced something of a mental breakdown in returning to civilian life so abruptly. As part of his recuperation, he went to his brother's farm where, among other physical activities, he built a sturdy range of kennels -- still in use a half-century later. John remembered that it was not long after his father returned home that he began work on a more modest version in the backyard at Sheringham, a single kennel with a fully enclosed wire-mesh exercise yard.

The day Prince arrived was one of John's happiest memories. By then John was eight, almost nine, years old. Yet he realised that his recollections of Prince, a pure-bred black Retriever, were almost as blurred as

7

Prince's nameless predecessor -- but for an entirely different reason.

John recalled that just as Johnny in *Shadow the Sheepdog* did not take lightly his training responsibilities, so he too had devoted himself to this bright-eyed, loose-limbed, energetic creature, the veritable "Black Prince" of his youthful imagination. Memory can lend a roseate hue to the past and in John's mind's eye, that was a glorious time in his young life.

Under the supervision of an older cousin, John would take Prince for long training sessions over the windswept golf-links, situated high up on the cliffs overlooking the North Sea. Prince proved to be an easy dog to train, was not messy like the mongrel, and even seemed to enjoy the grudging regard, if not altogether undisguised affection, of John's mother. John's only regret was that unlike the characters in so many of his children's books, he was never allowed to have Prince sleep on his bed, nor even in his room. His mother was very clear about that. His father had built the kennel especially for Prince and that was where he lived. Dogs, it was drilled into John, have their place.

Then came the day that was firmly etched in his memory, the day that his parents told him that Prince was dead. In today's world of veterinary practice when puppies are vaccinated almost as routinely as human babies, it is hard to conceive of the terrible toll that Distemper used to take. Otherwise healthy dogs could be taken sick overnight and simply waste away with this cruel disease. At that time there was no cure. John couldn't recall when he first knew that Prince was one of its victims.

On that terrible day, significantly, the sky was leaden and overcast, not unusual for those parts, and John had just got out of school. There, standing at the school gateway, were his parents. Since his father always worked late he knew immediately that something was dreadfully wrong. Explaining that they had just come from the Vet's and the reason why Prince "had to be put down" (a chilling phrase, surely even to an adult), they urged him not to cry, to be brave, and to accept that it was "all for the best".

There was no talk of getting another dog. The kennel and run were dismantled and that portion of the garden was given over to a lawn. John never had another dog as a child. Not long afterwards, or so it seemed, he learned that a cure had finally been found for Distemper. In any event, his aunt's dog Bingo, a not particularly endearing mutt if ever there was one, subsequently survived a bout of Distemper and went on to live a goodly seventeen years.

John wondered if perhaps something had died within him all those years, because on the plane travelling between Miami and Toronto, he experienced a numbness, a constricting of his insides, which seemed to choke any attempt at tears. That had certainly not been the case when Tuppence had died two years previously. Returning home from the local animal clinic after having had her put down, the tears had gushed freely then as he and Karen had united in grief.

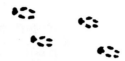

Tuppence, a black and white English Cocker Spaniel, was really Karen's dog. She had owned her since she was a six-week-old puppy, having first made her acquaintance when Tuppence was little more than the size of her hand. Tuppence was five years old when she came into John's life on July 1, 1988, taking up residence in their cramped one-bedroom apartment on the eighth floor of an old high-rise in Milton in southern Ontario.

Karen and John were in the process of having a townhouse built in Mississauga, closer to Toronto, which they would be moving into in a matter of months. However, before they even had time to discuss their changed circumstances with the building's ever-vigilant superintendents, they were served with an eviction notice. While it appeared the superintendents were prepared to turn a blind eye to the many unofficial felines in the building (perhaps because their own daughter had one), allowing anyone to keep a dog was definitely contrary to the rules.

Determined not to give cause for actual complaint, John began the practice of walking Tuppence up and down the back stairs rather than to use the elevators. That same night his bond with this little creature was really cemented.   Frightened by the sound of all the firecrackers that were being let off in the nearby park in celebration of Canada Day, she fled the basket they had set up in their bedroom.   John found her crouched abjectly behind the toilet in the bathroom, whimpering forlornly.   Until the fireworks ended he stayed with her, trying to quietly comfort her, his hand tucked companionably through her collar.   Next morning he took her to work with him.

In those days, John, a Probation Supervisor, was based in a small office located on the second floor of a shopping mall.   Tuppence, at twenty-five pounds, was small enough to be carried comfortably, so he had no difficulty sneaking her up the back stairs and into his office where he was able to settle her down beside his desk.   As time went by Tuppence became an accepted and popular occupant on the second floor and the need for furtiveness decreased.

Part of John's responsibilities included super-vising four satellite offices.   Like most dogs, Tuppence loved to ride in the car so it became his habit to take her with him whenever he visited those locations.   As they would make their way down the different corridors John would hear staff exclaim: "Hello!   Here comes JR and Tuppence!" as her jangling Name and Rabies tags gave advance warning of their impending arrival.

Since Karen at that time worked in downtown Toronto, a daily round trip of forty miles, by default Tuppence spent more time with John than her.   It was not unnatural, therefore, that he should take proprietary interest in, and start to view Tuppence as, his very own dog. It had taken almost forty years but finally he had joined the ranks of proud dog owners. He had a dog again, one that could now sleep in his bedroom and could even sleep on his bed (as she so often did when she knew John and Karen had gone to sleep).

The threat of eviction passed. Within only days, it seemed, the superintendents moved to another building and their successors, knowing that John and Karen would be also leaving shortly, did not press the issue.

With the move to the town house in Mississauga, they decided to get a cat to keep Tuppence company during the day since, with a pending job change, John knew he might not enjoy the same latitude of having a dog in his office. Fiona, little more than six weeks old when they got her, joined the household the second day they moved to Mississauga. She bonded quickly with Tuppence, the latter begrudgingly tolerating the kitten's antics.

Five years passed. The two animals became part of the firmament. But of course present patterns of life don't go on forever. It was evident that Tuppence, by now ten years old, was indeed going grey but then, John acknowledged ruefully, so was he. It was with real shock therefore that, steadfastly believing Tuppence had at least another four years of healthy life ahead of her, they learned that she was gravely ill. Even then, it was not until they got the results of the bone-marrow biopsy confirming myeloid leukaemia that they bowed to the inevitable. When the time came John held her in his arms as she was mercifully "put to sleep". Despite Fiona's presence their home felt dreadfully empty.

Lianne and Paul, who had by this time acquired Paisley, a, handsome, good-natured Chocolate Labrador, suggested John and Karen immediately get another dog. For both of them it was too early. They had a four-week vacation in South America coming up and, in any case, they had decided not to get another English Cocker Spaniel. One of Tuppence's not so endearing traits was her tendency to snap at, and indeed bite, young children. All attempts to discourage this behaviour had been to no avail and John and Karen had subsequently learned that Cockers were ranked as the worst offenders in this canine category. Nevertheless they were still attracted to Spaniels and so when Lianne, not so subtly left them her copy of *Dogs in Canada* to peruse, they turned to the section on Spaniels. Which is how they came to get Dylan...

Chapter 2

Early Days

Dylan started life with the name of Buddy. That was the "call name" he was given by Gerry and Nancy Curry who had by then been breeding Spaniels for more than ten years. Dylan was one of a litter of five pups born to Penny, a sweet-tempered dog with the beautiful rich red and cream coat that sets Welsh Springers apart from other breeds of Spaniel. Of all his three brothers and sister, he most closely resembled his mother in his markings. His father, who belonged to another owner, was born in what is now the Czech Republic. According to family lore, he had been smuggled out of that country as a tiny pup in the deep pocket of his owner's raincoat.

Dylan's puppy days were much less adventurous. The shyest of the bunch, he tended to stay close to his mother, never exhibiting the same curiosity as the others whenever friends of the Currys dropped by to see the latest litter. The Currys lived out in the country, northwest of Hamilton, a large industrial city on the southern shores of Lake Ontario. On weekdays, Nancy made the long commute into Toronto to teach at an inner city elementary school. Gerry, a self-employed computer consultant, worked out of their home, so the dogs were rarely confined to the kennels at the back of the house.

Under the supervision of Penny, the pups were permitted considerable freedom to play in the large meadow beside the house. So it was not long after they were born that the pups ventured outside. It didn't matter whether it was hot or cold or even teemed with rain because Welsh Springer Spaniels are blessed with what dog fanciers describe as "an all-weather coat". They could be literally drenched to the bone, their fluffy chest and leg feathers flattened and their creamy white markings obscured by black mud but within a half-hour of being back inside the house, their coats would be back to normal. Their body hair is so fine that it is just a matter of time before any mud dries and simply drops off. A not so good characteristic, however, is that they shed hair just as easily.

As is the practice with most breeders of pedigree dogs, the Currys already had prospective owners lined up for the pups long before they were born. One by one Dylan's three brothers departed with their new owners, each putting on a brave face as his turn came to leave his mother. Dylan knew he was next. As the lone female, his sister Allie was going to stay with Penny and the Currys so that they could breed her.

In the days that followed it was inevitable that Dylan and Allie grew closer. Of the two, Allie was by nature the more lively and inquisitive. Whereas Dylan would always tend to hang back, she was never afraid to explore and was usually the one to initiate their rough and tumble play. Cuddled up together at night in the familiarity of the homely kitchen in which he had been born, Dylan would have been quite content to remain with Allie and Penny for the rest of his life. Indeed, when the people who had asked for him never showed, Gerry and Nancy talked about keeping him for themselves.

But Dylan's world began to change when Karen telephoned the Currys, enquiring about Welsh Springer Spaniels. She told Nancy that she and John had read about them in *Dogs in Canada*. "Could we come and see your dogs?" she asked.

The afternoon they visited, Dylan as usual hung back. It was Allie who allowed them to pick her up and fondle her while Dylan stayed as far away as possible, hiding under the table. As she petted Allie, Karen told the Currys that she had always preferred bitches. In any event, within the next two weeks she said they would be going on vacation to South America for a month so that Dylan would be five months old by time they returned. This would be long past the usual time for new owners to take possession.   If Dylan was listening, he must have heaved a sigh of relief.

Back in Mississauga, however, Karen couldn't stop talking about Welsh Springer Spaniels. That same night she telephoned the Currys again. Despite Dylan's gender and shyness, she said that she had taken a real fancy to him. Now she asked: "If he still has not been claimed by the time we return from our holiday, could we please have him?"

Gerry and Nancy, like all genuine breeders, are selective when it comes to choosing owners for their pups.   In John and Karen, a couple then in their early fifties, they recognized good dog owners; people who really care for their animals and understand their responsibilities when it comes to proper feeding, grooming and the need for regular exercise.   Without hesitation, Gerry responded: "He's yours when you return".

Few new owners keep the "call names" that breeders give pups.   When Nancy asked John and Karen what they were thinking of calling him John replied hesitantly: "Maybe Glamorgan, Morgan for short -- in recognition of his Welsh ancestry".

So while John and Karen were on their travels, in preparation for his new home, the Currys began to wean Dylan away from Penny and Allie and to address him as Morgan. It was only while John and Karen were up in the high Andes, touring the mysterious Inca settlement of Machu Pichu, that Dylan got his name. As part of his holiday reading material John had packed several dog-training books. A fellow traveler, a retired surgeon, happened to notice the books and asked what kind of dog they had. John explained that they were getting a Welsh Springer Spaniel on their return, not yet really named. Their companion, himself a dog-owner who hailed from Wales, rejoined enthusiastically: "Oh you must call him Dylan – after the poet Dylan Thomas."

John and Karen looked at each other and agreed immediately: Dylan it would be. From then on, whenever they talked about what they would do when they returned home, Dylan was always part of the conversation...

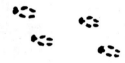

True to their word, the day after they got back from South America they wasted no time in claiming him. If he was disconcerted by a second change of name the shy pup did not seem to show it. Resigned to his fate, he submitted to being installed in a crate that the Currys lent John and Karen until they purchased their own. Indeed Dylan displayed little interest in his surroundings until he arrived at the townhouse in Mississauga. Left to his own devices to sniff around, it was not long before he identified a clearly non-human smell – that of Fiona.

Fiona had missed Tuppence dreadfully. Immediately following the dog's death Fiona would wander the house plaintively, indicating her loneliness by more than usual unsolicited affection towards John and Karen.   Mindful of Dylan's timidness and the need for him to establish himself in his new surroundings before connecting with his new feline companion, John and Karen had deliberately delayed collecting her from the kennels. They reasoned that Fiona would be so glad to be back home that she would likely be more accepting of him if he was already there when she arrived.

Their animal psychology proved to be sound. Although initially startled by the presence of the gangly pup in her home, Fiona seemed to size him up in seconds and, as expected, took charge. Any thought she might have had of letting slip one of her "trophies", her usual rebuke for John and Karen's temporary abandonment, was forgotten.

Within hours Fiona had formally adopted him and literally had him under her control, acceding to her every whim.   Such was her power, that over time she trained him to literally wash her ears.   No matter that he might be resting quietly, she would make her way over to him and thrust her face towards him for the proffered lick. Then, arching her back and almost swooning in the evident physical pleasure it brought her, she would encourage him to lick her ears until both stood stiffly to attention.   As for Dylan, he nearly always complied, licking valiantly until she padded haughtily away.

In those early days, Fiona undoubtedly provided much needed fellowship for the shy pup.   Although house-trained, any new encounter with other dogs or strangers inevitably resulted in a flood.   John and Karen's veterinarian, aware that Dylan was five months' old when they got him, expressed concern regarding his shyness and doubted his ability to successfully bond with them.

Tuppence had always slept in a basket in the bedroom and from the first day John and Karen continued this practice with Dylan. He was also not discouraged – if anything the contrary! – from climbing onto their bed for a cuddle. With Karen being away so much because of the demands of her job it was natural that John became Dylan's prime figure, his *alpha*. He was clearly John's dog, hugging closely to his heels, and John delighted in his devotion.   John was concerned, however,

20

lest Dylan become a one-person dog, so his basket was moved to Karen's side of their bed. It did not take long before Dylan became as much Karen's dog as he was John's.

Socializing him to other dogs as well as people was also an initial concern, so they made a point of introducing him to strangers -- human and canine. As for their Vet's experience that shy dogs tended to be biters, from the outset Dylan was trained not to snap if a hand was put in his food bowl. Indeed, so placid was he in this regard, that Fiona regularly got into the habit of helping herself to one or two bits of bone meal every meal time. Within two weeks, Dylan's incipient nervousness had diminished almost completely.

With all the pride and enthusiasm to be expected of a new dog owner, John wrote the Currys: "Well, we're coming to the end of our first fortnight (the most difficult period, I believe you said?) and, as his Report Card indicates, he's a solid member of our family, i.e. we feel he's just right." Enclosed was John's fanciful rating:

Progress in socialization	B+
Adjustment to new environment	A+
Acceptance by feline	A
Bonding to new pack	A+
Response to direction	B+
POTENTIAL	A+++++

Dylan was introduced to formal obedience training at seven months. By this time John had trained him to return a thrown ball, so at "show off" time at the end of the course this was his special trick, earning him a merit ribbon. Dylan learned to keep to "Heel" (well, sort of) and to follow hand signals to sit and lie down. When directed to "Stay" for more than a minute, however, he was less obedient. Much like a trained circus dog left to his own devices, John found that when he turned his back Dylan would immediately stand up and cautiously begin to follow. John had read that Welsh Springers were reputed to have a sense of humour and this practice seemed to him to be Dylan's unique way of pulling John's leg.

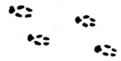

Everyone needs a friend, especially when growing up, and Dylan was no exception. Fiona might be company when his owners were at work but most of the time she kept to herself. In any case, their relationship was always on her terms, whenever she was inclined to be sociable. In those early days when the young pup would seek her out she would more often than not disdainfully ignore him, removing herself to a chair or sofa knowing full well that it was out of bounds to him.

Fortunately it was not long before Dylan connected with Paisley, the gregarious Chocolate Labrador, belonging to Lianne and Paul. Within days of John and Karen bringing Dylan home, the two dogs were formally introduced -- and immediately became fast friends. More than a year older and considerably heavier, Paisley nevertheless still had plenty of playful puppyness in him. His friendly, gentle nature belied his solid bulk. It was not long before each could be roused to excitement by the mere mention of the other's name. Whenever John or Karen would say: "We're off to see Paisley", Dylan would immediately become alert and start looking around expecting to see his friend. Lianne and Paul reported a similar reaction from Paisley.

At that time Lianne and Paul lived in the west end of Toronto, within easy walking distance of Etienne Brulé Park, one of several public green spaces that border the Humber River. It became a regular practice for the two couples to meet up for long walks with their dogs. Paisley had already become an extremely competent ball retriever. In Dylan he was delighted to find keen competition. Both dogs would literally quiver with excitement whenever they thought there was a ball to be hunted down, and both became quite expert, after lots of false starts, at distinguishing feigned throws from the real thing.

Despite Paisley's heavier build, Dylan was no match for the older dog in those early days. With a passion bordering on fanaticism, Paisley would take off at breakneck speed, anticipate the ball's bounce and then race back, pursued all the way by an adoring Dylan who was usually running interference like a football player. To this day, Paisley becomes quite demented when he knows that someone has a ball. As long as there is a ball to be thrown, he will chase it. John has often expressed concern that the big lab could drop dead before he would give up. Indeed, keeping up with both dogs' demands sometimes became a chore. So when throwing over arm became too stressful, Lianne took to using her tennis racquet. It was a practice that John also adopted.

But it was the mock fights with Paisley, in which each uttered bloodcurdling yowls and looked as if he was about to tear the other to shreds, that Dylan seemed to enjoy most. They would roll around, first one the aggressor with the other at his mercy, snapping mock ferociously at the prone dog's throat, before reversing roles. Then inspecting each other minutely as dogs invariably love to do, they would finally settle down quietly, content to be in each other's company. As they grew older, the ferocity of this play ritual mellowed considerably, though usually one would still try to invoke the other into a full-scale rough-and-tumble.

Whereas Paisley was Dylan's best friend, it did not mean that he did not develop other canine friendships. Across the road from John and Karen's home are school playing fields and a small public park -- a popular locale for neighbourhood dog-owners to exercise their pets. It was here that Dylan became acquainted with Carter (named after the Toronto Blue Jays second World Series home run hero), Taffy (so shy and meek that Dylan seemed aggressive by comparison), and Tara (extremely territorial whenever another dog came anywhere near her owner's property). All three were Golden Retrievers, a breed with which Dylan usually enjoyed an immediate rapport.

His canine friends also included Floyd, an aristocratic Rhodesian Ridgeback and Daphne, a butterball American Cocker.   Though other dogs, including Carter who outweighed Floyd by several pounds, tended to avoid the strong, wilful Ridgeback, for some reason Dylan was never afraid of him.   Indeed whenever Floyd's and Daphne's owner, Robert, engaged in a mock fight with Floyd, pretending to fend him off, without fail Dylan would come to Robert's defence, growling at Floyd to desist.   As for his relationship with Daphne, she became ecstatic whenever she saw Dylan, gazing up at him with adoration and licking him lavishly on the mouth. Daphne also shared his enthusiasm for ball chasing, charging after him, panting and puffing, never conceding an inch. On the occasions when she did get possession of the ball, however, she would race away proudly and have to be coaxed to give it up.

Through visits to Chris and Delia's farm property, Dylan also got to know her dogs, Fritz, an irascible Daschund, and Phantom, a shy, fleet-footed Retriever-cross.   Dylan's relationship with the Daschund was perfunctory. Typical of the latter's breed, he was extremely independent-minded, tolerating Dylan with a Teutonic disdain that seemed to brook no argument as to Dylan's place in his pecking order. In contrast, Phantom tended to defer to Dylan, except when it came to chasing a well-thrown ball. Then she was poetry in motion, displaying an extraordinary agility in leaping into the air to snatch a ball -- a trick that Dylan later copied.

Thus, much as he might have missed Allie, his mother, and the familiar surroundings of his early months, it was not long before Dylan settled into the routine of his new life. So secure had he grown in his new relationships that John and Karen were somewhat surprised when on a visit to the Currys some three months after his leaving there, Dylan seemed almost distant from Allie and Penny, hardly having anything to do with them. If anything he tended to keep close to John and Karen all the time they were visiting, evidently concerned they might leave without him...

Chapter 3

Unsettling Times

The expression "It's a dog's life" has always had a pejorative note about it. Yet surely for most dogs in western societies the reverse applies. As beloved family pets, a dog's life usually means a stable home, at least two meals a day and lots of exercise. Routine is not a negative word; rather, when their routine becomes disturbed, animals, especially sensitive ones, become unsettled. All of which perhaps explains how Dylan came to be on the run.

In the Fall of 1995 John and Karen both worked for the Ontario provincial government. A few months earlier there was a General Election and because of electoral promises made by the incoming Conservative Party, overnight, Karen's job became threatened. John was already planning to take early retirement within the next two years with the prospect of their possibly moving to a country location.

When Karen was offered another position in Orillia, a smaller community some eighty miles north of Mississauga, she therefore jumped at the chance of a full expenses paid move. Within days of receiving notification of the position, they had visited Orillia and scouted the area for a home. Of course Dylan travelled with them, his senses keenly alert to all their stress as they traipsed through different properties for sale. They finally settled on a new bungalow, on two acres of land, which they felt they could transform into their dream home.

In the meantime Karen had begun work in Orillia. Rather than make the long drive daily she elected to stay over during the week, a situation that neither she nor John found easy. Back in Mississauga, they listed their townhouse for sale. Day after day Dylan and Fiona had to contend with a stream of prospective buyers coming into the house. In those days it was still John and Karen's practice to leave Dylan in his crate while they were out of the house. Both the real estate agents and their clients made a point of commenting how Dylan sat so quietly, seeming to take everything in.

Animals can be very sensitive to human vibrations and if anything Dylan had always been a little too sensitive. John Phillips, author of *The Essential Welsh Springer Spaniel*, notes that "Welsh are most responsive to nuances and slight changes of voice and facial expression, and of everything else." Dylan hated raised voices and if he sensed that John and Karen were starting to argue he would slink out of the room. To induce him to return they would both have to call him. Then hesitantly, his eyes anxiously glancing between the two of them, only then would he come back. Under the circumstances, it is little wonder then that Dylan would have been extremely unsettled by the atmosphere of anxiety and uncertainty that hung like a dark cloud over John and Karen's home in the Fall of 1995 -- especially when John too found himself job-threatened.

With government down-sizing the order of the day, John learned that a management position was being eliminated where he worked so even though he had been a government employee for more than twenty years, he would have to compete for his own job against two fellow supervisors. Complicating matters further was the fact that John and Karen were scheduled to shortly take a long-planned four-week vacation in South Africa. Seasoned travellers, they fleetingly considered cancelling the trip particularly as it was becoming doubtful whether Karen's new position was going to be permanent. As the time edged closer to their departure, John fortunately managed to hold onto his job.   The likelihood of Karen's being confirmed in the Orillia position, however, appeared to be growing slimmer.

And now there was another wrinkle.   The previous year when they had gone abroad, Dylan had stayed with Lianne, Paul, and Lexi.   Despite being close to term with a second pregnancy, Lianne had been prepared to have Dylan stay with them -- that was until Paul, fast-rising in the computer software industry, was offered a major position in Ottawa.   Faced with all the disruption of having to put their house on the market and packing up all their belongings, Lianne not unnaturally felt she could not cope with an extra dog for four weeks.   Reluctant to leave Dylan in kennels that long, Karen asked Delia to have him stay with her.   The sisterhood is strong in Karen's family so if Delia had any concerns about this last minute arrangement, she hid her feelings.

The day before John and Karen were due to leave for South Africa Lianne offered to take Dylan overnight, saving them a trip into downtown Toronto.   She said she would take Dylan to her aunt's the next day.   It was then, without pretending to be in any way psychic, that John did have some misgivings about their leave-taking of Dylan.   So while on their travels, whenever Karen, who does sometimes have psychic moments, would express her concern ("Do you think Dylan's alright?"), John's too-confident assurances masked an inner uncertainty.

But the excitement of the pending trip, the need to cancel the house-listing, it being one less thing to worry about, and the recognition that despite all her

30

efforts to determine otherwise Karen would not know whether she had a permanent job until their return, all combined to push any foreboding to the back of their minds. Despite all the uncertainties on the home front, they were going to South Africa on a meticulously planned tour, designed to take them from Johannesburg via Kruger National Park, Swaziland and Zululand all the way down to the Cape with a special side trip to Victoria Falls. For the next four weeks they were going to forget about work, their family in Canada, and try to take in all they could in Nelson Mandela's exciting new "Rainbow Nation."

The next day, as John and Karen were beginning their long transatlantic flight, a harried Lianne was fighting rush-hour traffic to deliver a puzzled Dylan to Delia's house. If he had been bewildered before as to where he was going to be staying, now he was really confused. Hardly had he arrived at Lianne's home then he found himself being carried into the garden at the back while Lianne did some paint touch-ups, preparatory to the arrival of their Real Estate agent. The following morning, he was bundled into the family mini-van for the drive to Delia's house. With Paul away in Ottawa and all her energies directed towards having to get their house ready for viewing, Lianne could not be expected to worry about an upset dog. To make matters worse Delia was in the midst of making arrangements for a party that night, so Dylan found himself being somewhat unceremoniously deposited in the boot room along with a could-not-care-less Fritz and a diffident Phantom.

"I didn't feel good about taking him to Delia's," Lianne said later. "I literally had to leave him at the door, but I had so much going on. I had to be back that night to get ready for the first of the salespeople coming through the house."

Normally she would have stopped in for a cup of tea and a chat with her aunt. She left behind an obviously discomfited Dylan. That night he whined so piteously that Delia, knowing he slept in John and Karen's bedroom, did not have the heart to leave him downstairs. For the rest of the night he wandered around the house, his nails clicking on the wooden floors to the annoyance of the rest of the household trying to sleep.

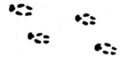

Meanwhile John and Karen were glorying in being back in Africa. En route to their hotel, their eyes were drawn to the tin shacks in the distance marking the creeping suburbs of South Africa's fastest growing city, Soweto. Later that week they would have an opportunity to visit Johannesburg's former South West Township, now better known by its acronym, and to learn firsthand that it is much more than a collection of poverty-stricken hovels. Rather, it is a cosmopolitan community with vast sections of middle- and upper-class residences, has its own university, is home to the largest hospital on the continent, and to people living in neighbouring black totalitarian states, the mecca for thousands of illegal immigrants. It is also the site of the 1976 massacre of school children protesting against apartheid. Today a memorial, unveiled by Nelson Mandela, stands on what used to be part of the school playground. Little did John and Karen realize as they absorbed these impressions of an all too recent stain in South African history, that a small drama was unfolding a continent away.

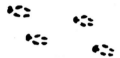

Delia and her husband Chris own a recreation farm in Grey County, two hours north of Toronto. It is a marvellous place for dogs with lots of opportunity to run freely, not to mention a host of wonderful smells. Dylan had stayed there several times and, had he not felt so disconsolate, would ordinarily have welcomed the prospect of taking off for The Farm that weekend, but yet another twist entered into the saga of events precipitating his big adventure. Prior to going to The Farm, Delia had accepted an invitation to stay the night with a friend en route. Taking her own two dogs as overnight guests was one thing; bringing along a third, particularly one in such a despondent mood, was simply out of the question.

Once again, therefore, a downcast Dylan found himself abandoned as Delia, Fritz and Phantom drove off leaving him in the care of Mary-Lou, her dog-sitter. If Dylan's spirits had begun to rise in the last few days when it became clear that he was going to stay at Delia's, they now sank to a new low. The leaden skies and cold chill in the air betokening an early winter mirrored his gloom.

Near where Delia and Chris lived is Chorley Park, deceptively large with its heavily wooded slopes which further north become the Moore Park Ravines. It is ideal for long rambling walks with dogs requiring lots of exercise. It was almost a daily routine for Delia to take Fritz and Phantom there. Dylan, of course, was included and had begun to enjoy his frolics with Phantom. But it was a different story the morning of Saturday, October 21...

DAY 1

Mary-Lou found an apathetic animal moping around the kitchen. His tail between his legs, Dylan allowed himself to be led to the park, uncharacteristically showing little interest in his surroundings. Once away from the public paths and reaching the open meadow that stretches into heavily wooded ravines, Mary-Lou, as per habit, unfastened his lead

For the slightest fraction of a minute Dylan stood stock still. Dog and human regarded each other. It was only an instant but it seemed considerably longer. Dylan's stare was impenetrable yet Mary-Lou intuitively glimpsed his intent. "It was as if he was telling me, I'm out of here," she said.

Seeing the alarm in her eyes, even before she had time to reach out and grab his collar, Dylan turned and began to trot determinedly away. The transfixed Mary-Lou recovered her composure and gave chase but the fleet-footed dog merely increased his pace and sped off. All Mary-Lou could do was to watch helplessly as he was swallowed up in the leafy darkness of one of the ravines. She spent the next hour walking the park and calling his name, all to no avail. She did not even get a sighting. Dylan had totally vanished.

Hoping that he might have made his way back to the house, Mary-Lou retraced her steps. There was no sign of him. When after another hour he had still not returned she called Lianne. With Paul home for the weekend, Lianne was trying to take advantage of his presence to attend to a bevy of chores, more plentiful then usual because of the demands of readying the house for sale. Dropping everything, Lianne, Paul and Lexi drove to Delia's house taking Paisley with them in the hope that he would prove a lure for Dylan.

Chapter 4

First day on the run

Dylan was feeling in much better spirits. It was as if a huge cloud had lifted, dissipating his feelings of depression.   His keen eyes quickly adjusting to the ever-changing light breaking through the still leafy canopy of the trees on each side of the ravine, he found himself luxuriating in all the woodland smells, made more heady by the damp air.   As any child knows, freedom from adult restraint can initially be an intoxicating emotion.   Since dogs live in the present without heed to consequences, Dylan was in his own world.

How the homing instinct in dogs works is a mystery. Enough anecdotal evidence has been accumulated however to suggest that it is no chance factor. So when Dylan took off from Mary-Lou that morning his intent was single-minded -- to be reunited with his owners, however long that would take. What he could not know was just how formidable a task this would prove. Mississauga lies immediately to the west of metropolitan Toronto, Canada's largest city.

As the crow flies the distance between Chorley Park and his home in the west end of Mississauga is only some thirty miles, but as with any large metropolis the terrain in between presents a very different picture. Toronto sprawls around the south-west shore of Lake Ontario, its downtown core a mass of high-rise office buildings, with residential and industrial development all around. Parkland tracts, usually beside ancient river beds, often running at the foot of sometimes surprisingly deep ravines, dissect the latter. Many, such as Chorley Park, have dense woodlands.

At first Dylan found the going easy. The ravine that he had entered, though steep in places, was a natural corridor, the trees and undergrowth effectively shutting off any human distractions. Within seconds, Mary-Lou's frantic entreaties to come back had been blotted out, replaced by the tranquil sounds of the natural habitat -- the sibilant whisper of leaves rustling in the trees, the crackle of dead leaves underfoot and the occasional sigh of the early winter wind.

Whether by breeding or temperament, Dylan had always been easily distracted. So when a squirrel darted directly in front of him, without a second thought, he gave chase.   Unused to having to contend with predators at that time of day, the startled squirrel hesitated for a fraction of a second before instinctively fleeing to the nearest tree where it scurried up the trunk.   From the safety of a branch well out of reach, its chest still heaving, it watched bemusedly as the dog below made half-hearted efforts to leap up.   Whenever he was off leash and had the opportunity, Dylan had always enjoyed chasing squirrels.   He had never caught one, indeed had never come close, and what he would have done, if he had been successful, was anyone's guess. But as long as there were squirrels, Dylan would continue to chase them no matter how tired or dispirited he was feeling.

Satisfied that the squirrel was not going to provide more sport, Dylan stopped prowling round the tree and turned his attention to the exciting smells all around him. Dogs experience a sensory world in which smell predominates. Their ability to distinguish different smells many miles away, provides them with a very different landscape to humans -- one made up of many layers of distinctly different scents, some so powerful that were we humans, to be similarly endowed, it is likely that we would be overcome with nausea. Dylan, on the other hand, was in his element; it was like being back in the woods at Delia and Chris's farm.   He was totally oblivious, at least temporarily, of the circumstances that had resulted in this unexpected, but most welcome, freedom.

Who knows how long he would have continued to meander had not the terrain suddenly changed.   As abruptly as his idyllic journey had begun so now the woods gave way to human habitation, bringing him back sharply to the reality of his situation. Whereas before his pace had been unhurried, now he began to trot, exhibiting a purposefulness that suggested he was familiar with his surroundings; a neighbourhood dog returning to his home. After all, he was wearing a collar with Name and Rabies tags indicating clearly that this was no stray. So the few people he encountered, their heads bent forward to protect them from the by now driving rain, hardly gave him a second glance as he continued his path south.

The traffic in Toronto is generally lighter on weekends but to a shy animal, unfamiliar with clanking streetcars and a steady stream of vehicles of all sizes, it must have been chaotic. Cars and trucks raced by in a whirling maelstrom of harsh metallic sounds and gasoline smells. Nevertheless he continued to press forward, ever watchful of the traffic hurtling by.

Dylan became especially cautious after one near scrape with a city bus which swung dangerously close to the sidewalk as he was about to cross. Thereafter, wherever possible, whenever negotiating a street corner, he would sidle over to a group of pedestrians waiting for the lights to change and, as unobtrusively as possible, attach himself to one of them until the crossing had been made. In most instances the person never even noticed him. In this manner he worked his way efficiently from street corner to street corner until finally he found himself looking into what seemed like a long tunnel, the underpass near the large downtown railway station.

Lengthening his stride, Dylan ran into the gloom only to emerge a minute later at the foot of another huge structure -- the Gardiner Expressway, the raised highway which runs south of the city's downtown core, parallel to the lakeshore. With vehicles streaming up its ramps and constant traffic rumbling along the six-lane road underneath, it presented a tumultuous and scary scene. The cross-sections are controlled by traffic lights but unlike those he had previously encountered there was not the same press of pedestrians, affording brief islands of safety. For most of the time the traffic flow appeared unbroken, as vehicles using the ramps made right turns on red lights.

If there was ever a Guardian Angel taking care of Dylan, this had to be one time when her munificence was taxed. Only she would know for sure how he was able to make that particular crossing unscathed. But one thing is certain: within three hours of taking off in Chorley Park, Dylan was on Lakeshore Boulevard -- making his way steadily west towards his home in Mississauga, some twenty-five miles away.

Dylan was plodding along the shore path at what is known as Palace Pier, an old Toronto landmark, when he became aware that he was the object of attention of a man out walking his dog. Harry Birkman is a lawyer who lives in one of the high-rise condominiums that occupy prime waterfront locations. Normally he leaves the city on weekends but on this day he was walking his dog in his own neighbourhood.

By this time Dylan's pace had slackened considerably. He was tired, the pads on his paws sore from the constant contact with the hard pavement. He wanted to stop and rest but felt driven to continue. Harry could see that despite his bedraggled appearance, he was clearly a pure-bred. He had a collar and rabies tag so obviously he was someone's pet.

But whenever Harry tried to approach Dylan, the dog backed away. No amount of coaxing would encourage him to come forward. Eventually Harry decided to take his own dog home and return with some biscuits, figuring he could lure Dylan close enough for him to grab the dog's collar. After Harry and his dog departed, Dylan relaxed his guard and found a spot under some bushes where he curled up for a rest. But he had hardly closed one eye when he realised that now two more men had become interested in him. They too began to try to entice him to come to them, but Dylan was having none of that and ran off.

It was then that Harry returned and together the three men began stalking the nervous dog, trying to surround him. Tired though he was, Dylan led them a merry dance for the next two hours. Every time they tried to entrap him, he managed to move just far enough away to avoid capture. At one point they thought they had him cornered.   With a feint that would have done a professional football player justice, Dylan slipped past all three men leaving them clutching at thin air. . "He led us a merry dance, but he was just too smart for us", Harry said.

A steady drizzle which was beginning to turn to rain was made more unpleasant by the cold wind coming off the lake.   It was sufficient to encourage all three men to decide to call it quits.   The last Harry reported seeing him, Dylan was still heading west.

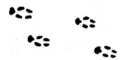

Meanwhile in Chorley Park, the little search party, not surprisingly, had drawn a blank.   With Paisley leading the way, Lianne and Paul had set off with Lexi in her stroller.   Whistling and calling Dylan by name they tramped through the park.   The afternoon drizzle had gradually turned to pouring rain so they were all soaked by the time they abandoned the search that evening. Back at Delia's house, the mood was grim when Lianne telephoned Delia at The Farm to tell her what had happened. Delia promised to return the next day to join in the search.

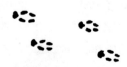

A continent away, John and Karen had just returned from visiting Victoria Falls in Zimbabwe and were now touring Soweto and Gold Reef City, the latter the site of the country's first working gold mines and now a tourist attraction. Karen, who had some psychic proclivities and who has never been afraid to speak her mind, now started to express her misgivings about the way they had taken their leave of Dylan. It was to be a frequent refrain during the remainder of their stay in South Africa. "Do you think Dylan's alright?" she would ask. "Of course," John would retort, somewhat exasperatedly, undoubtedly because, if truth were known, he was feeling decidedly uncomfortable himself. "After all he's stayed with Delia before -- and he loves The Farm."

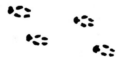

Whether he was unnerved by the chase at Palace Pier or had second thoughts about what he was doing, will never be known. But as night fell in Toronto, Dylan began to retrace his steps, all the way back to the vicinity of Chorley Park, a round trip of more than twenty-five miles. By now he was hungry and tired, the pads on his feet scuffed from walking so long on the unforgiving pavement. It had been a long day and he was both physically and emotionally drained. Although he had always been a house pet, being fed and cared for, Dylan now drew on his heredity for survival.

Welsh Springer Spaniels are not a particularly common breed in Canada. Dylan's ancestors reputedly date back to Roman times, when the Celts (the early Welsh people who resisted Roman rule) first used them for hunting. With their soft bite, Welsh Springers make excellent retrievers; until fairly recent times they were mainly kept as working dogs and restricted to their native Wales. With their all-weather coats and ability to withstand extreme temperatures, they were popular working dogs. It explains perhaps why Dylan was not particularly distressed by the chilling temperatures as night drew in and he found himself outside overnight for the first time in his short life.

Compared to other domesticated family pets, he was perhaps better equipped than most to cope with the uncertainties of an open-air existence. Nonetheless his equilibrium had clearly been upset. Bewilderment at his change of status, tempered with his natural timidity when confronted with so many strange sights and sounds, now drove him to keep a low profile, slinking silently along the dark city streets, deliberately avoiding human contact. His experience that afternoon on the lakefront had obviously disposed him to distrust strangers, however well meaning and kindly. By the time that night he curled up into a damp, bedraggled ball in the by now familiar ravine-lands, he had already started to shed some of his domesticity.

Chapter 5

The search begins in earnest

DAY 2

Sunday, October 22 was another cool, damp Fall day. Lianne and family, accompanied by two friends and their dog, drove over to Delia's house to join Mary-Lou in renewing the search.   With Paisley again leading the way, the little party trudged through the park, whistling and calling Dylan's name. Ever the modern day businessman, Paul was in the midst of a long-distance call on his cell-phone when he was interrupted by Paisley barking furiously. A bemused client in California was then treated to a full explanation of what was happening 2,500 miles away.   As it turned out there was no foundation for Paisley's excitement, so once again after tramping for what seemed like many miles in Chorley Park, they had to give up the search. They went back to Delia's house to find that she had returned early. Paul had to fly back to Ottawa that night and so began the three-week-long Delia-Lianne "Dylan Watch".

Dylan had gone to ground.   After his night in Chorley Park, he had made his way north of where he had parted company with Mary-Lou into what is known as the Moore Park Ravines. By now he was beginning to feel quite hungry, not having had anything to eat for 24 hours. With the pads on his paws bruised from all the pavement pounding they had undergone the previous day, he was quite content to stay in hiding. It was late in the day when hunger drove him to forage for food, finally lighting on a nearby schoolyard. There his sharp nose detected a possible food source -- an enticing smell, emanating from a

46

garbage can with a loose-fitting lid.   It took him almost twenty minutes, pawing and scratching, to get the lid off, but not before he had toppled the can on its side with a resounding clatter.

Momentarily startled, he had immediately sprung away, his eyes darting nervously in all directions.   But no-one was around at that time of night on a Sunday so, satisfied that he would not be disturbed, he returned to the garbage can and scavenged its contents.   Apart from a half-eaten hot-dog, the pickings were slim.   To make matters worse, in his efforts to pry off the garbage can lid, he had suffered a bad cut to the pad on his right front paw.   It was therefore a woebegone figure who returned to the ravines to find a secure resting-place for the night, eventually settling on a long-vacated fox den where he spent the better part of the next day only emerging occasionally to take a sip of water from a nearby puddle.

DAY 3

Delia is a no-nonsense, down-to-earth person who is fiercely loyal to her family.   Starting that Monday morning, she swung into action.   She wasted no time in contacting the Toronto Humane Society and all those in the city boroughs and neighbouring communities including Mississauga and Oakville.   "It didn't take long to discover that they all have different practices when it comes to handling Missing Dog enquiries," she said.   "I established first name contacts so that I could call them back according to their different posting procedures."

Photocopying a recent photo of Dylan, Delia then made up more than a hundred posters and recruited her friends in the neighbourhood to put them up on lamp standards and hydro poles. She also made up copies to give to all the local schools for distribution. That evening, Lianne, having returned from a day's teaching and having settled down Lexi for the night, telephoned Delia to plot their next move. It was to become their regular routine for the next three weeks. One thing they agreed; no good would be served by contacting John and Karen while in South Africa.

On that first Monday morning John and Karen had joined a German-Dutch tour group heading up into the Drakensberg mountain range of the Eastern Transvaal. Late that afternoon they stopped at Pilgrim's Rest and it was in this gold prospector's village that they first learned of the saga of Jock of the Bushveld -- the story of the exploits of a legendary bull terrier immortalised by his owner, Sir Percy FitzPatrick, in what has become a South African children's classic.

In the little museum at Pilgrim's Rest, John learned more about the benighted FitzPatrick family. Tragically, all three of Sir Percy's sons died in their twenties. The eldest was killed in World War I and it was Sir Percy who suggested to the British Parliament that two minutes silence should be observed on November 11 to commemorate the deaths of all those who had died in the cause of freedom, a practice that has now been adopted world-wide.

Whenever they travelled abroad, John bought books often indigenous to that particular locale, so buying Sir Percy's book seemed a natural thing to do. Meanwhile Karen, the real shopper in the family, had spotted an ornately decorated leather dog collar. John knew Dylan was never far from her thoughts. His picture was included in her "Grandma's Brag Book", a small photograph album which she delighted in showing to their fellow travellers. Now turning to John she once again said: "Do you think Dylan's alright? I do get concerned about him." They bought the collar. It was the only occasion on any of their travels that they ever purchased something for their pets.

Dylan had surrendered to sheer exhaustion. Coiled up in the former fox den, he was able to escape from his new reality. The blood from the cut on his forepaw had congealed, though all four pads were still tender from the unaccustomed bruising they had experienced padding along the Toronto streets. Though hunger was beginning to gnaw at his insides, instinctively Dylan knew that rest was what he needed most at this time. Through occasional forays to a nearby puddle, he satisfied his thirst. Careful now not to draw attention to himself, he nonetheless had let down his guard once. Believing himself alone, he was lapping thirstily in the puddle when he was somewhat disconcerted to find himself under the scrutiny of a baleful Boxer whose owner, he noted, was looking inquisitively in their direction. Backing away, he retreated to his lair where he remained for the rest of the day.

Dusk had fallen when he set forth again in search of food. He found the garbage can still on its side, its contents now spread across the playground thanks to the probable activities of a racoon and, judging by the lingering smell, a skunk. Whatever crumbs of food there might have been, had long since been devoured. He carried on, all his senses alert, transformed into a creature of the night. But after an hour of scouring the neighbourhood of the school, he abandoned his quest, returning to the familiarity of his den.

That night he slept fitfully, in sharp contrast to his first night in the open, when exhaustion had plunged him into a deep sleep. Now he was acutely aware of all the noises of the night: the wind in the trees; an owl twittering from a branch in the big oak whose roots formed part of the den walls; the calls of the different night hunters. His mind was suffused with memories. Conscious of his damp coat he was reminded of the vigorous rub-downs he received in the garage back home after an especially wet morning walk; the combing he half-heartedly acceded to, particularly those times when his ears were heavily matted; and even more clearly the closeness he experienced to his owners at those times. And, of course, after every morning walk, there was a bowl of food waiting for him. Memory of the latter made him acutely aware of the emptiness of his belly and his present circumstances. With dawn starting to break, he finally stirred. Stretching his lithe frame, Dylan once again set off south, but this time in a slightly more easterly direction towards the Don Valley.

The Don River, which flows through the valley that bears its name, is situated in Toronto's east end. The Don Valley Parkway, the six-lane highway that meanders along its eastern shoulder, is clogged with traffic almost 24 hours daily. In sharp contrast, down in the valley itself, it is a different world. Apart from the occasional building, the flood-plain has changed very little since the coming of the first white settlers.   Whereas the terrain did not afford as much cover as in Chorley Park, the dearth of human activity meant Dylan could relax his guard somewhat as he continued on his journey.

DAY 4

By now word had spread throughout the neighbourhood and Delia had received reports regarding the first of several sightings. At Lianne's suggestion she had also begun visiting neighbourhood schools. She particularly appreciated the reception she received at Whitney Public School. "I had gone there to put up a poster and the Principal invited me to write up a message for the morning announcements. Then she handed it to a Grade 6 girl to read over the PA system." Delia said. Everyone she spoke to was sympathetic but no-one reported seeing a stray dog. Outside in the playground, the garbage can which had been lying on its side for a few days had finally been righted and its lid clamped tightly shut.

Dylan meanwhile had spent the day travelling at a comfortable pace along the Don Valley, taking care not to arouse attention from the few people he saw in the distance. For much of the time, he was content to follow the Don River as it wound its way southwards to Lake Ontario. Despite the onset of winter, the foliage in the valley was still dense enough at this time to afford him a degree of camouflage so that he could travel quite leisurely without fear of detection. The pads on his feet were no longer sore, but the memory of that first day on the run was still fresh. He had no intention of returning to the hustle and bustle of the city streets unless absolutely forced to do so.

Passing under a huge viaduct, one of several bridges that span the valley, Dylan happened upon the detritus of a drinking party held the night before. Amongst all the empty beer bottles, an untidy pile heaped in the scrub grass, lay two large take-out pizza boxes, each containing three slices. Judging from the number of beer bottles and caps, those who had participated had consumed more liquid than food. After determining that he was clearly alone, Dylan tucked into this unexpected feast with gusto. Finding a food source so easily may have led him to decide to hunker down in the Don Valley for the night, because when the light started to fade Dylan found himself a sheltered hollow and curled himself up to rest.

DAY 5

Delia was putting up notices at the bottom of Chorley Park, stopping everyone to tell them about Dylan, when a young man on a bicycle said: "I think I saw the dog you were looking for." He volunteered to cycle the whole park circuit. Delia held her breath but when he returned, it was to report that he had had no luck.

Beth Marley, who lives in Delia's neighbourhood, was one of those who actively joined the search. Her interest was particularly piqued because she is the owner of two Welsh Springer Spaniels and for the past nine years she had exercised her dogs in Chorley Park. "I wondered if Zoe and Cai would lure him out of hiding but we never did

see him," she said.   "Lots of people gave my dogs some
hard looks though! "

DAY 6

In their travels, John and Karen had entered
the mystical kingdom of Swaziland, a principality often
described as the Switzerland of Africa because it is
ringed by mountains on all sides.   Like most small African
countries it is quite poor.   But out in the countryside the
people live proudly in rondavels, the distinctive African
round wooden huts with conical-shaped roofs, selling their
handicrafts at makeshift roadside stands.

Somewhere along the way Karen had learned about
the famous Swazi candles, particularly those designed to
provide a stained glass effect when only the inner core
burns.

"Would any-one else be interested in going to the
Swazi Candle Factory?" she enquired.

The candle factory had not been a scheduled stop on
the tour itinerary.   Nearly all the men in the group
indicated that they were quite happy to give it a pass but
the womenfolk had different ideas.   By the time the tour
party departed from the candle factory, its stock had
been greatly depleted with each member of the tour party
having purchased at least a couple of candles.

DAY 7

Despite the worsening weather Delia had taken to her bicycle to comb the neighbourhood.

"I cycled for three weeks. I was in the best shape I'd been in for years"!), she later acknowledged (this from an individual who is perpetually slim!)

Interspersed with all her bike riding were long walks in the Chorley and Moore Park Ravines, following up any sightings, which meant that Phantom also got lots of additional walks during this time. Immediately north of the Moore Park Ravines is the old city cemetery. Given all the initial reports she had received of Dylan having been seen north of Chorley Park, Delia thought there was a good chance he might have ventured into it.

"Phantom and I walked up to the Mount Pleasant Cemetery which is huge," she said. "We went to the administration building and I talked to the gardeners and handed out posters. They were all very sympathetic and promised to keep an eye out since no dogs are allowed in the cemetery."

Dylan, however, had now taken up temporary residence in High Park, the large inner city park in the west end. After spending a couple of nights in the Don

Valley he had made his way past the railway shunting yards, where the Don Valley Expressway connects with the Gardiner Expressway, and travelled some of the route he had taken the first day he took off. But instead of proceeding west beyond Palace Pier he had turned north into High Park which afforded him more cover as night began to fall.

By this time his coat had lost its sheen and he was noticeably thinner. After his first experience with the garbage can in the schoolyard, he had become adept at scavenging, including sometimes driving off the occasional alley cat whose territory he had invaded. He had been almost faint with hunger the first time he happened on the kitchen of an Italian restaurant.

Seeing the shy dog, straining to sniff at the cooking smells, one of the cooks who was standing in a doorway taking a smoke-break, tossed him some scraps which he devoured greedily. Throwing caution to the wind, Dylan came closer and was rewarded with more tidbits before an imperious voice from within demanded that the cook get back to his duties. Unfortunately, Dylan's system was ill-prepared for this sudden feast and he was subsequently violently sick. But he had learned a valuable lesson -- and from then on he kept a close lookout for restaurant kitchens.

Chapter 6

One week turns to two

Each day Delia would return from extended walks, hoping to find a message on her answering machine advising of Dylan's whereabouts. In addition to listing her telephone number, the posters offered a reward for his safe return. Meanwhile there were also reports of sightings in High Park, west of the Toronto downtown. Since John and Karen were in the habit of regularly exercising Dylan with Paisley in Etienne Brulé Park, which is not far from High Park, Lianne thought that there was a good possibility that Dylan had made his way to High Park looking for Paisley.

DAY 10

After a particularly busy day at work, Lianne picked up Lexi from her baby-sitter and found a message on her answering machine saying that there would be a showing of their home at 6:30 p.m. that night. In the midst of quickly (that is, "as fast as a woman who is seven months pregnant can") vacuuming the house, feeding Lexi, and tidying up, the phone rang. It was Delia calling to say that a stranger had just phoned, reporting she was sure that she had just seen Dylan in High Park. Perhaps, her aunt thought, Dylan was making his way across the city to Lianne's home. "Could you check it out?" she requested.

Lianne wanted to get out of the house for the Real Estate showing anyway. She set off with Lexi and Paisley. When they reached the park they were met by two women, sisters, who pointed out where Dylan was last supposedly seen. Hollering for Dylan, they made their way into the darkening night as a light rain began to fall. Lianne put Lexi on her shoulders and let Paisley off the leash, hoping he could draw Dylan out of the darkness.

After a fifteen-minute walk and no sign of Dylan, the two women decided to head home, the opposite direction to Lianne's parked mini-van. Lianne thanked them and headed back to her vehicle through the deserted park. Then it struck her. Usually a cautious person, she couldn't believe the situation in which she had placed herself and her young daughter. She was in the middle of a large inner city park, in the dark, in the rain, seven months pregnant, carrying a crying, tired toddler and with only a very licky and friendly family dog for protection. Her stress level peaked at that moment as her imagination began to run wild; she said her heart started to race. She picked up her heels and ran and didn't stop running until she got to her mini-van.

Back at home, she found a message on the answering machine from the Real Estate agent. The showing had been postponed until the next day. "I hope you didn't go to too much trouble," the message concluded. Lianne called Paul in Ottawa and started to cry. A long day at school, the search in vain for a lost dog, futile house-cleaning, the demands of being a single parent and a rush of pregnancy hormones hit her like a blizzard. The way she was feeling, she was unsure as to how she would have reacted if she had found Dylan. As she told Paul, she thought she would either break down and cry (because she would be so overjoyed to see him), or she would get so mad that she would grab him by the neck and beat the stuffing out of him for what he had put them all through. It did not help her mood when Paul, in comforting her, laconically observed that Dylan was probably on a veranda somewhere, getting a good feed and having a great time...

Dylan's situation was much less idyllic. Adapting to his new habitat, he had become almost invisible. Travelling in the half light of early morning, he had inconspicuously wended his way until he reached familiar territory -- Etienne Brulé Park. The sight of the arches of the stone bridge there evoked warm memories of times spent gambolling in the park with Paisley. They had spent so many joyful hours together, chasing after tennis balls and plunging in the shallows of the river. But now with the cold winds, hinting at an early winter, the park seemed a much less welcoming place.

In vain, Dylan tried to locate Paisley's scent, not knowing that the big dog's long walks of late had been spent in Chorley and High Parks looking for him. Indeed they had missed each other by a matter of hours, Dylan having again retreated south after having been alarmed by the intense scrutiny he had received from the two women in High Park. Now in familiar territory, he recognized some accustomed canine faces (or rather their scents). But when some of their owners displayed a little too much curiosity for comfort, he moved quickly away, slinking into the undergrowth. He remained in Etienne Brulé Park for two days, much to his disappointment, never once catching a glimpse of Paisley.

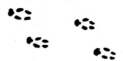

John and Karen were by now travelling along South Africa's famous Garden Route, the highway with spectacular views which runs along the east coast between Port Elizabeth and the Cape. Seven bridges, some being magnificent feats of engineering and design, span deep gorges while proteas, South Africa's unique national flower, grow profusely by the side of the road. But even though they were thoroughly enjoying the scenery, their thoughts these past few days had been about Canada. This, after all, was late October 1995, when Canada was gripped by the prospect of Quebec separating.

It was John and Karen's practice to travel in the Fall but invariably something important happened on the home front while they were away. Avid baseball fans, two years previously they were in South America when the Toronto Blue Jays clinched their second successive World Series title. Once again they found themselves out of the country at an even more critical time, anxiously grabbing at any bits of information they could glean in regard to news from back home. Fortunately the South African news media, freed from its apartheid era censorship, carried extensive coverage, likening Quebec's independence aspir-ations to those of Zululand-Natal.

John and Karen were staying in Knysna, midway along the Garden Route, when they tuned into CNN in the early morning hours of Halloween to catch the live broadcast of the Quebec Referendum results. South Africa is six hours ahead of Eastern Standard Time, so they were able to breath a collective sigh of relief at the same time as their families and friends back home were -- that they would not be returning to a fractured country.

DAY 12

While visiting the old Dutch Cape Colony capital of Swellendam, John and Karen's tour group bumped into a party of French Canadians. Impulsively Karen raced up to them and volubly expressed her joyous relief that Quebec was still part of Canada. Then, realising that they might not share her sentiments, particularly after the narrowness of the vote, she pulled back. Fortunately they were federalists. Despite Karen's mused misgivings from time to time about Dylan's welfare, they had no reason not to believe that all appeared to be well with their world as they continued on their journey to Cape Town for their final week in South Africa.

Etienne Brulé Park is just one section of a network of both small and quite large parks which border the Humber River. Concerned about the continuing attention he was receiving from one man who seemed to be tracking him, Dylan headed north following the Humber River as it threaded through what is known as Lambton Woods and Scarlett Mills, crossing under Highway 401 (which is twelve lanes wide as it runs through the north end of the city). Emerging from the long river tunnel he continued to head north into what he found to be almost deserted parklands except for the usual wild life. It was here that Dylan was to experience one of his worse moments, a chance event which would change his behaviour forever...

DAY 14

It was little more than a lean-to, a rough wooden frame shack in the woods that clearly had seen better days. The roof had started to cave in and most of the glass in the solitary window was cracked, with whole sections having fallen out, and the remainder only held in place by an ancient screen. But the door, a sturdy affair, still hung on its hinges, swinging gingerly whenever there was a slight gust of wind. Dylan approached cautiously. The temperature had dropped sharply and the first wisps of snow were not far off. He shivered involuntarily. The state of being constantly on alert, combined with a lack of food, gave him a gaunt appearance. Shelter from the chill of the night would be very welcome.

Satisfied there was no sign of human activity, he poked his head round the door and sniffed. It was deserted. The only furnishings in the small, one-room structure were a rough wooden table near the window and a rusted metal folding chair. Two spiral ring notebooks, some pencil stubs and a book with a worn and faded cover lay on the table. A page of barely discernible bird illustrations hung on the wall by the window, secured by two thumb tacks.

If he had hoped to find food, Dylan was clearly out of luck. Given its isolated location, the shack had likely been used as a bird-watchers' hide and judging by its unkempt state, it had been abandoned for some time. Not only that, he found evidence to suggest that he was not the first creature to seek sanctuary there. Under the table, against the wall, was a collection of feathers and some bones. His predecessor, likely a fox, had clearly dined as well as rested there. Dylan settled for a warm bed for the night as the wind began to howl ever more insistently.

He awoke with a jump two hours later, startled by the slamming of the door in its frame -- the result of an extra sharp gust of wind, penetrating the broken window. The impact was such that the door latch, a rusting heavy cast iron device, was jolted and fell into place, firmly securing the door and thereby trapping the hapless dog. Dylan was not immediately aware of his changed circumstances, preferring to cuddle back down into his warm bed and resume his interrupted sleep.

Awakening just before dawn, however, he quickly realised his predicament when he tried to depart the way he had entered. Vainly he scratched at the door, attempting to disengage the old latch, becoming more agitated the longer he tried. Conceding defeat, he started to pace the room hoping to discover a hole in the wooden walls that he could enlarge. Once again he was unsuccessful. That left only the window. Climbing onto the table he began to attack the screen with his forepaws, scratching furiously at the metal mesh. Despite its age and condition, there was no indication that it could be moved.

His front paws sore from his efforts, he jumped down from the table and resumed his pacing around the hut, his agitation rising by the minute. He hated the feeling of being trapped. After being loose, on his own for so long, he could not abide confinement. The once-comforting walls of the shack now appeared to be closing in on him. His warm bed under the table lost its glow with the spectre of continuing imprisonment. Half-heartedly he tackled the door again, scratching and clawing vainly at the latch mechanism. Then he resumed his distraught pacing.

The sun was well up in the sky when he again focused on the window as a means of exit. He climbed back onto the table and this time he charged at the window, throwing his full weight at the screen. He was rewarded by the sound of some wire strands popping and the screen bulging under the pressure. He again flung himself at the screen and was once more rebuffed, but not before more of the mesh wires had snapped. Encouraged by this success, he continued to hurtle himself ever more vigorously at the screen until a hole began to appear on the left side.

Summoning up all his strength Dylan now launched himself full tilt at the window screen. With what seemed like an unearthly tearing sound, the screen gave way and Dylan found himself sailing through the opening in a shower of broken glass. He landed in a heap on the ground, temporarily winded. He was immediately conscious of the pain coming from his right hip, the site of a score of open wounds caused by small glass shards and the needle-point ends of the fractured wire mesh as they raked that side of his body. But all he could think about was that he was free again, free to pursue his quest.

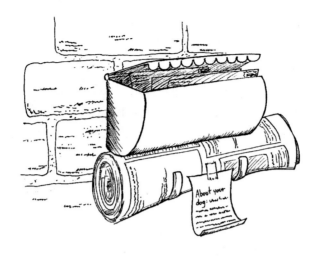

Chapter 7

The weeks pass

One week turned to two, two weeks turned to three, and still no sign of Dylan. That did not stop Delia thinking of him day and night. She would dream that he was at the front door and several times got up, each time around 3:00 a.m. to check. She explained that her dreams were especially vivid because of an experience she had had several years previously. At that time another of Delia and Karen's sisters who lives close by in Toronto had a Dalmatian named Cassidy.

Apparently one night Cassidy, upset by the painters then working in her owners' home, took off and made her way to Delia's house, arriving after Delia had retired for the night.   A neighbour who had a key to the house recognized Cassidy sitting on the front door mat and let her in.   Cassidy made her way up to the bedroom and Delia recalled "smelling wet, old dog" and thought she was dreaming about her long since dead dog Corfu.   The next morning she was astounded to find Cassidy at the foot of her bed.

"So you can understand why I got up so many times in the night hoping by some miracle to find Dylan on my doorstep," she said.

Delia had also by now enlisted the help of the Toronto garbage truck drivers.   She reasoned that they were usually out early in the mornings when a stray dog might be easily spotted.   In the same vein she spoke to the woman who delivered her early morning newspaper.

DAY 18

After touring the Cape area, which included ascending Table Mountain by the steepest cable car they had ever ridden in, John and Karen had set off to see the Bushmen.   The Kagga Kamma clan, a tribe of the dwindling and only known surviving Bushmen group in South Africa, then resided at The Cedarberg, a land of breathtaking craggy red rock formations some eighty miles north of Cape Town.

At the time of John and Karen's visit, this clan of pure-bred San, much like aboriginal peoples in many other countries such as Canada, were awaiting the outcome of an historic land claim that would see them return to a hunting-gathering lifestyle in the desert. The tribe had moved to their present location, a private game reserve four years previously after being forced off their land in the Southern Kalahari for illegal poaching. Whereas these once nomadic people had made a home in The Cedarberg, it was clear that their hearts were still in the Kalahari, the land of their forefathers. A few years later, in a precedent-setting decision, they won the right to go back to the Kalahari Desert to live.

DAY 21

When Delia went to her front door to pick up her morning newspaper she found a note attached from the woman who delivered it, stating simply: "I've seen all kinds of racoons but not your dog." Meanwhile, acting on the adage that "no news is good news", Tricia, the friendly Scottish woman at the Toronto Humane Society who had become an almost daily confidant, tried to reassure Delia that *Dylan* must still be alive. "If anything had happened to him, if he'd been struck by a car, we would surely have heard by now," she said. "If he was dead we would have found his body."

Delia was not so confident. "I had written him off", she said. She knew that Chorley Park and the other ravines that bisect Metropolitan Toronto were vast. With the falling leaves and an early snow fall prevalent, she considered that the body of a forty-five pound dog could easily be hidden and not discovered until the following spring. Such a thought did not bear thinking about and both she and Lianne, during their nightly telephone vigils, comforted themselves with the hope that someone had found him and that he was now being well cared for.

As the days rolled by, until John and Karen's return, their not unnatural anxiety was the couple's reaction to the news of Dylan's disappearance. After much deliberation they decided that Paul should be the one to break the news. While agreeing to take on the unpleasant task, Paul, who likes to tease, was concerned that Karen and John would think he was joking.

DAY 23

All their planning became irrelevant when Karen decided to call from Miami and it was Lianne who answered the phone. First topic of conversation was Lianne's pregnancy, and how she was faring. Then Karen asked about Lexi and next they talked about how the sale of the house was going. It was only then that Karen enquired about Dylan. Poor Lianne burst into tears and blurted: "Dylan's been missing for three weeks." Lianne said she thought she was going to get through the conversation until that point. As for Delia, she deliberately did not answer the phone that first day John and Karen returned.

"I just couldn't face telling you," she later told her sister.

By the time their plane landed at Toronto's Lester B. Pearson International Airport, to be met by Lianne, Lexi and Paisley, John and Karen had managed to compose themselves. The last thing they wanted to do was to upset Lianne further. Hard as it had been to receive the news in Miami, at least they had had an opportunity to digest the information, work through their shock and, albeit tentatively, begin to make some plans.

The drive home seemed strange. In the past Lianne had brought Dylan to the airport to greet them, always the first step in reassembling their little family. As Lianne recounted all the events of the past three weeks, John sat silently in the back seat. It was all such a bad dream and all he could think of was the smart leather collar, tucked away in his suitcase, that Dylan was now never going to wear.

When Lianne and company finally left, the house seemed dreadfully quiet and empty. Dylan had never been a noisy dog, barking only when someone came to the door. His absence was chilling, and his empty basket in the bedroom a constant forcible reminder. John and Karen clung to each other, Karen weeping uncontrollably. For reasons John could not fathom, he was dry-eyed, but his insides were numb.

They went to bed early, both waking after a troubled sleep, distinctly believing they could hear whining. The feeling was so strong they felt compelled to open the front door to dispel the wishful belief that a familiar figure was at their doorstop, asking to be let in.

71

DAY 24

Their second day home, a Monday, was a holiday for government employees.   Karen was scheduled to fly to Sault Ste Marie later the same day, beginning the first of five weeks of staff training that she would be delivering in Northern Ontario.   She had set up these sessions prior to going on vacation, not knowing what her status would be on their return.   She intended to spend the morning doing vacation laundry and catching up on housework.

Normally John would have pitched in but on this morning, even though he knew it was useless, he wanted to go to Chorley Park, to see for himself where it had all happened.   John loathed driving into Toronto at the best of times.   That morning it was snowing and the traffic was backed up so he left the expressway at the first opportunity and started cutting through the residential streets to Delia's and Chris's home.

Over the years their elegant old city home had been a haven for many younger family members while attending college or starting out on their own.   Interspersed with relatives have been other young people, who in return for having the use of a well-appointed basement apartment at a nominal rent, were expected to feed and exercise Chris and Delia's dogs and cats when they were both away. Lianne spent a year there while attending teacher's college.   Mary-Lou was the most recent guest/tenant. Delia, Chris and Mary-Lou were all still at home when John arrived, Delia having delayed her early morning walk with the dogs.

She did not have to be told that John's visit that morning was meant to try to bring closure to the terrible burden of responsibility she felt because of the circumstances surrounding Dylan's disappearance. With Phantom leading the way, Delia and John walked the short distance from her home to Chorley Park. Unlike the postage stamp size park and school playing fields where John exercised Dylan each morning, once in the heavily wooded ravines he saw that they could easily have been far out in the country rather than in the heart of Canada's most densely urban and populous metropolis.

At the start of their walk John would whistle and call Dylan's name but deep down he knew he was wasting his time. He was simply going through the motions. It was all too easy to understand how Dylan had been lost in the extensive system of ravines and valleys which border on Chorley Park. After three weeks it was clearly hopeless to expect to find him there now.

Back at Delia's house, John retrieved Dylan's leash and other reminders of his last stay there and drove home to Mississauga. When John later dropped Karen off at the airport, he couldn't help but note the anguish in her face and the droop in her shoulders.

Chapter 8

Almost home

Some time around the third week of his remarkable journey, and about the same time that John and Karen were first learning of his disappearance, Dylan finally made it to Mississauga. The city, which takes it name from the Indian tribe who lived there in pre-Columbian times, is only about twenty-five years old. Yet as a new, planned city, it is now the second biggest in Ontario and the sixth largest in Canada.   Originally comprising almost a dozen distinct communities, it stretches from the Etobicoke River, the border with Toronto, in the East to Oakville in the West. In the north east it is home to Lester B. Pearson (Toronto) International Airport while in the north west the former villages of Streetsville and Meadowvale have been swallowed up in recent years by considerable residential and industrial development.   Farther south the one-time villages of Port Credit and Clarkson directly front the shore of Lake Ontario.

After his abortive forays in the different Toronto parks, Dylan had again set a south-westerly course following Lakeshore Boulevard, the original main thoroughfare between Toronto and Hamilton which hugs the shoreline.   By now almost indifferent to the constant roar of the traffic on the nearby throughways, he loped steadily on, wherever possible using underpasses to avoid crossing the multi-lane highways.

Sweeping, in ever widening circles, comes naturally to Welsh Springer Spaniels.   By this time, moving back and forth, he had already covered the distance between his home in Mississauga and Chorley Park many times over. After several days meandering in the parklands along Etobicoke Creek, his scavenging skills now significantly developed, he arrived early one evening at Port Credit, the mouth of the Credit River.   Erin Mills, where John and Karen lived, lies immediately south of Streetsville through which the Credit River flows, and some eight miles north of the river mouth.   John and Karen had never traversed its full length but prior to leaving for South Africa they had taken Dylan for a walk along the section near their home, at times forcing their way through what was often chest-high natural growth. They planned one day to explore further down-river.

Now, perhaps instinctively knowing that home lay somewhere north, Dylan once again turned in that direction, following the river bank. Unlike his experience in the Humber River marshlands, he found the going comparatively easy along the Credit. He settled into a steady lope, all his senses on auto-pilot. In this vein he continued for about seven miles up-river when he became aware that he was not alone. Dusk was fast beginning to fall, creating large pools of menacing shadows. Emerging into a small glade, he was startled to find himself the subject of intense scrutiny by two unwavering grey eyes.

Almost involuntarily, Dylan came to an immediate stop, his heart pounding vigorously. There was something extremely sinister about the other creature that now began to stealthily draw forward from the lengthening shadows that until then had cunningly concealed him. With relief Dylan saw that it was another dog, likely an Alsatian-cross. He usually avoided this breed, but at least he knew what he was dealing with; that was, he thought he did. But as the other animal continued to approach ever closer, Dylan's initial composure was replaced by dread, especially when it emitted a high-pitched yipping.

Like a jangling alarm bell all his senses screamed out; this was no ordinary dog. This creature had never experienced domestication. As its confidence proclaimed, this was clearly its domain and Dylan was now faced with the age-old predicament -- Flight or Fight.   That he decided on the latter likely came as a surprise to both the coyote -- as that is what the other creature was -- and to Dylan himself.   Although badly frightened, the Welsh Springer Spaniel had not come this far to give way so easily.

Teeth bared, with a blood-curdling yowl, he suddenly sprang forward. Taken by surprise, the coyote fell back, deftly dodging the dog's onrush. In attempting to snap at Dylan's neck, it tore the flesh in his left cheek as the dog sought to avoid what could easily have been a fatal thrust. With blood spurting profusely, Dylan was now transformed into as fierce an aggressor as his opponent. Snarling with a hitherto inconceivable ferociousness, he launched himself on the coyote, sinking his teeth into the other's neck, and hung on desperately.

The two animals, locked together, rolled over and over until finally the coyote tore free -- leaving Dylan still hanging onto a chunk of flesh. Immediately the coyote was back on the attack, again lunging at the dog's neck. Something primitive, however, had been awakened in the domesticated animal and he easily parried the other's assault, but not before the coyote had almost gouged Dylan's left eye with its sharp teeth. Fortunately Dylan had lowered his head at the last second and the coyote's lunge had torn the flesh above the eyebrow. As blood began to pour from this second wound, Dylan became aroused into even greater ferocity.

The noise of the battle and the scent of fresh blood did not go unnoticed. Unbeknownst to Dylan, two other members of the coyote's pack had been drawn to the scene by the coyote's earlier quavering yelps. Now they stood watching silently. Their first inclination had been to join the fray, but something about the intensity of the one-on-one struggle induced them to hold back. Generally, small and even medium-sized dogs are no contest for coyotes but in this instance it was clear that the combatants were evenly matched. Their eyes and heads darting keenly as they followed the action, the other coyotes elected to sit back on their haunches and watch.

Normally Dylan weighs in at around forty-five pounds but his weight had dropped considerably over the previous three weeks as he scavenged to feed himself. Unlike some of his more pampered Spaniel brethren, he had never been one to carry excess weight. With his dull coat, still matted with blood from his escape from the hut and his obvious terror when first confronted, he must have seemed easy prey to a coyote familiar with the habits of domestic animals.

With the continuing growth of Canada's cities, inexorably penetrating into ancient woodlands, humans and coyotes are now living in closer proximity than ever before. Yet true to their Indian descriptor as "ghosts of the forest", coyotes are rarely seen between dusk and dawn when they forage for food, slinking silently through fields and hedgerows and increasingly along public footpaths and into residential backyards.

Under the unblinking attention of the other coyotes, Dylan and his adversary tried to savagely break down each other's resistance. No sooner would one draw blood then the other would retaliate. Snapping and snarling, thrusting and parrying, they rolled on top of each other, neither giving an inch. Whereas Dylan's wounds looked uglier, it was the coyote, however, which had sustained the more serious injury. The area of its neck, from which the skin had been so brutally torn away exposing bulging neck muscles, presented an inviting target to the determined dog. Repeatedly Dylan struck back at his would-be assailant's mutilated flesh until it was the coyote, clearly weakened from the tremendous loss of blood, who pulled away. Curling its large bushy tail between its legs, it turned and fled.

The other two coyotes shifted uneasily. Dylan, now fully aware of their presence, his faced blooded from both his own and the wounds inflicted on their companion, glared back defiantly. Undoubtedly, if they had attacked, Dylan's grand endeavour would have ended tragically on the banks of the Credit River -- little more than a mile from his home. But after what seemed like an eternity, the two coyotes rose and trotted off up-river, in the direction taken by their wounded brother.

Weak from his wounds and the loss of blood, Dylan was content to fall back to the south -- returning to the familiarity and relative safety of the Lake Ontario shore-line. Whether he knew just how close he had come to home will never be known.

Chapter 9

Where can Dylan be?

John found returning to work difficult. Everyone wanted to know how the holiday had gone. The response was hardly what they expected. "South Africa was great! It was coming home that was the downer." And, of course, he would then have to explain about Dylan.

Delia had given him her list of contacts so it was now his job to follow up with all the Humane Societies which after the first set of calls he made seemed to be a fruitless task after all this time. One telephone contact that day did provide some comfort. With his experience of the temperament of Welsh Springer Spaniels John wanted to know from Gerry Curry how long he thought Dylan might stay out before he became so hungry he would allow himself to be taken in by someone. "Perhaps three, four days," Gerry ventured. It was sufficient to galvanise John into action.

Lianne had suggested that perhaps John and Karen might try to contact all the veterinarians and animal clinics in Toronto to alert them in case Dylan was brought in for treatment or, in future months, a rabies shot. Her rationale was that he was an uncommon breed, that anyone giving him a home, assuming they were responsible owners, would sooner or later surely take him to a vet; he could clearly be identified from the large tattoo on his underside -- his Canadian Kennel Club registration.

Culling the Yellow Pages in the Toronto telephone directory, John came up with some 85 names and addresses. By the time Karen returned from Northern Ontario, the dining room table was littered with letters, enlarged photocopies of Dylan, and a pile of envelopes waiting to be stuffed, addressed and stamped. When Karen and John had first learned of Dylan's disappearance, they had felt completely helpless, believing that nothing more could be done. Now they felt more positive as they were doing something. This was assuming that he was still alive, and had not been spirited to another part of the country by professional dognappers -- a dismal thought.

On the employment front, Karen's prospects were equally gloomy. As she had suspected, the promise of a permanent position had evaporated and the word now was that within the month she would be officially declared surplus. Fortunately, John still had a job, in what had become uncertain times with the prospect of government-wide cutbacks and pink slips. While Karen and John were obviously pleased for Paul with his career advancement and the family's impending move to a much larger home in the Ottawa area, it meant yet another adjustment. The prospect of not seeing her eldest grand-daughter as often as she had up to now was yet another reason for Karen to feel sad as she kept her northern training commitment.

DAY 25

The fight with the coyote had clearly disoriented as well as exhausted Dylan. After leaving the Credit River where it joins with Lake Ontario at Port Credit in Mississauga, he had again struck west ending up for the night in a large public park, part of which at that time was given over to an extensive leash-free zone for dogs. Normally he would have been excited by the plethora of canine scents; now it represented a safe place to stop and to literally lick his wounds.

By this time he was a sorry sight. In the melee with the coyote, the earlier wounds he had sustained on his back and sides escaping from the bird-watching shack had opened and were bleeding again. His normally white under-body feathers were black, matted with dark blood. His left eye was almost closed with the torn flesh and congealed blood that had trickled down from the wound above his eyebrow.

If he had thought that he could settle in and be undisturbed for a day or two, he was sharply disabused of the notion early the next morning. Despite the increasingly wintry weather, a few hardy dog owners drove into the park with their pets for their usual morning exercise before heading off to work. At least two of the dogs came close to where he was hiding in some overgrowth -- too close for Dylan's comfort. Then possibly detecting the coyote's scent mixed in with that of the obviously blooded stranger, they moved off leaving him alone. Hours later, having attended to his wounds as best he could via a thorough licking, Dylan cautiously emerged. The park lies just south of the Lakeshore Road between Port Credit and Clarkson. Throwing caution to the wind, he took off like a rocket heading west along the shoulder of Lakeshore Road.

George Kloet, a Mississauga Real Estate salesman, was among those who saw Dylan streak by. He was standing outside his office when he first became aware of him: "My heart went out to the poor thing. He ran right through Clarkson village, past the GO [commuter] Train station. I saw people stopping and looking. People at the Bus Stop turned around to stare."

George said that by this time Dylan was running right on the road. "He was going at such a pace. Nobody could stop him. He was clearly on a mission."

George was so intrigued that he jumped into his car and tried to follow. He had almost caught up to the speedy dog at the city's border with Oakville when he was held up by traffic lights. By the time the lights changed, George had lost sight of him and had to give up the chase.

DAY 27

Dylan had become inured by now to the unseasonably cold weather. On several nights he had had to contend with below-freezing temperatures and frosty mornings. Given their proximity to Lake Ontario, Toronto and environs usually experience more moderate weather conditions than other parts of the province. But this year, snow had come early. Over six inches of snow had fallen by November 16, which was more than the area usually got for all of November. The day before, bitterly cold northerly winds had whipped up the first real snowstorm of the winter, causing havoc on the roads with dozens of fender benders. Many schools had also been closed. The next day another five inches of snow fell. Winter had indeed arrived with a vengeance.

For Dylan, however, the snow proved something of a blessing. Now he could create a safe, warm haven whenever he pleased by burrowing into a mound of light snow. With all the wounds he had collected, the need to lie low was paramount. Venturing out only to scavenge for food, he was more than happy to curl up in the snowdrifts near the lakeshore path. Until one day, that is, he was startled to find that his collar had caught on the slender branch of a young maple, bowed down by snow. Vigorously he tried to shake himself free but only succeeded in entangling himself further as the branch, cleared of snow through his efforts, sprung upwards half-strangling him.

Eyes bulging, Dylan was forced to stand on his hind legs to relieve the pressure on his neck, while his front paws flailed helplessly. Now completely panicked, Dylan swung his head to and fro, heedless of the pain caused to his windpipe as the branch sawed across his throat. Then just as he was starting to lose consciousness, something on his collar snapped and he broke free. On the ground lay his Name tag. It would be found with its broken hasp a few days later by Kathy Barnett who lives near the lakeshore in Oakville.

DAY 29

John and Karen's lives had slipped into a dulled state. Karen would begin to say: "I do hope Dylan's alright" and John would give her a pained look, aimed at forestalling further conjecture. Sensitive to their distress, one of Karen's sisters invited them to dinner in Toronto that first Saturday back. It was a bitterly cold and snowy night, and the roads were slippery, so they were in two minds whether to turn out. But feeling that life obviously had to go on, they accepted her kind invitation.

Karen has since remarked: "If I had known then that our beloved boy was out there", her voice quaking at the memory.

DAY 31

After his encounter with the coyote and his scare in the snow, Dylan had lost some of his appetite for being on his own. The half-completed housing developments then in progress south of the Ford Plant at Oakville seemed much more hospitable than some of the burrows that had been his resting place for the past month. An added bonus was that occasionally he happened upon workmen's half-eaten sandwiches, providing easily accessible snacks. He stayed in the area for four days. In order to fully sustain himself, however, he was required to range into downtown Oakville where he was spotted scavenging around the grocery store at the large town shopping mall. When one man showed particular interest and began to follow him, Dylan took off west towards the Glen Abbey golf course, the home of the Canadian Open.

Having a dog is like being responsible for a perpetual three-year-old. Cats have a capacity to fend for themselves and litter-boxes are worth their weight in kitty litter on stormy nights. If there was one thing in particular that brought home John and Karen's loss, it was the ritual of recycling plastic grocery bags. After unloading the groceries they would always fold the bags and store them in a hanging container in the hall cupboard in readiness for Dylan's next walk.   Though everything in his intellect screamed that there was little point in saving bags any more, John persisted in carefully folding and storing them as usual.

DAY 35

Dylan had taken up residence in yet another ravine, a habitat often frequented by coyotes. They were not the same as those he had encountered beside the Credit River and not the first he had seen since that incident.   They always kept their distance, studiously ignoring him. It was as if he had been clearly identified as a strange, crazy wild dog that should be best left alone.

Many anthropologists who study the different wild dogs in North America believe that coyotes have a surprisingly large vocabulary, much more extensive than wolves, and are able to communicate extremely effectively. Whatever the reason, the coyotes paid no heed to Dylan as they went about their nightly foraging.   This included the tracking and killing of several neighbourhood cats as was reported in the local paper that week.   One woman even related that she was attacked while out walking her small dog.   She had cried out at which point the coyotes had taken off.

In another newspaper report, Mississauga's animal control supervisor confirmed that the number of reported sightings in recent weeks was the greatest ever. Whereas it was highly unlikely that they would attack humans, he advised animal owners to keep an eye on their pets. He said that the "yipping and yapping" noises that coyotes made was typical, non-aggressive behaviour, but some coyotes were beginning to lose their fear of humans. Dog owners were therefore counselled to walk their dogs in daylight and to carry a flashlight.

"Travel with someone and (if you see a coyote) shine a flash-light in their eyes. Noise also scares them off," he said.

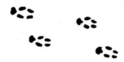

Sometimes on stay-at-home Saturday nights John and Karen rented movies for home viewing. It had become their practice to immediately take the video back to the rental store thereby affording Dylan a long walk before bed-time. That second Saturday night after their return, the walk to and from the video store was especially hard. Out of habit, each of them would catch themselves glancing down to look for Dylan, only to bitterly recognise their foolishness. At home Fiona would wander disconsolately, clearly puzzled and upset at Dylan's absence. She was not always one of the nicest cats but it seemed that she sensed their despondency and went out of her way to show considerably more affection than usual.

Chapter 10

Reunited at last!

The winter of '95/'96 will be remembered as long and extremely cold. On the night of Monday, November 27 driving back to Mississauga from all day meetings in Orillia prior to again flying north for training sessions, Karen experienced her worst moment.   That morning weather forecasters had predicted driving snow compounded by black ice and had advised motorists to stay home if at all possible.   Twice in driving down the three-lane major highway between Orillia and Toronto, Karen pulled over onto the side of the road because of restricted visibility as huge transport trucks thundered by.   As Karen has since told people about that time,

"I said to myself: 'This is crazy. John has already lost his dog. I can't have him lose his wife'".

Needless to say John's relief was palpable when he heard Karen's car pull into the garage that night.

If Karen was tense from her arduous drive, John was feeling equally strained because of the unsettling message he had earlier found on their answering machine when he returned from work:

"Mr. Roe.   This is Paula at the Oakville Humane Society.   Could you please call me at your earliest convenience."

John had had to contain his impatience.   When he tried to connect with the Oakville Humane Society it was to learn that it was a voluntary organization with limited staff hours.   John explained that he had a missing dog so it was critical he be told if it had been found.   The woman on the answering service, while sympathetic, down-played his anxiety and advised him to call back at 9:00 a.m. the next day.

"They often call back to check whether they should discontinue publicising an animal's loss," she said realistically.

Not knowing what to think, whether there was any substance to the call, John decided not to tell Karen as he feared raising false hopes.

DAY 39

Karen was scheduled to leave for Kenora for two days of training. Her flight was not until midday. For once it was an opportunity for a lie-in, rather than to have to jump up at the crack of dawn. But when John has something on his mind, sleep fails him, so he was up at his usual time, anxious to get to the privacy of his office telephone to make contact with Paula at the Oakville Humane Society.

He was in the office in good time that Tuesday, counting the minutes away until the clock struck 9 o'clock. Of course Paula was "not in yet" when he phoned. Perhaps, the person answering suggested, he could try again in a few moments? Try again he did, this time staying on the line until Paula finally answered. "Oh Mr. Roe. Thank you for calling. We think we have seen your dog. Does it have a white blaze on its nose?"

Prepared as he thought he was, John was stunned. Paula repeated: "Does he have a white blaze on his nose?"

John was shocked to hear himself blurting: "I don't know!"

Then, pulling himself together, he said: "Wait". Glancing at the photographs in his office he quickly confirmed: "Yes. He **does** have a white blaze."

Paula went on to explain that the dog they had spotted was wearing a collar, was quite thin and had been seen scavenging in garbage cans. When Humane Society workers had tried to put down food for him, he had run off.

"It's our opinion he's a panicked dog. Wally, one of our staff, has tried to catch him but he won't let anyone get close. Wally figures the only way we'll get him is if he gets himself trapped, perhaps in someone's backyard."

Could this really be Dylan, after all this time? John's mind was in a whirl.

"I'll be over," he said. "I'll bring pictures to see if we can make a positive identification."

John was scheduled to meet with a colleague to help him complete a major planning report. He telephoned him to tell him he would be delayed and why. Gérald has a dog of his own, so of course he understood immediately. After all it was Gérald who, while travelling in Europe a few years back, decided on the spur of the moment to call up his parents in Sudbury to inquire after his little dog Spartacus.

"Are you out of your mind?" his incredulous, irate father responded. "It's 2:00 a.m. here!"

"Forget that", Gérald said. "How's my dog?"

After having had to contend with John's gloom and lacklustre air since returning to work, his co-workers were somewhat relieved to see the sparkle in his eye even knowing that his new found excitement would likely be for naught.

Charging out of the door, John hurried to his car and drove the nine miles to Oakville. His birth certificate might validate that he was a greying mid-lifer but as far as he was concerned he might just as well be an eight-year-old boy again, looking for his dog.

The Oakville Humane Society's offices and pound are situated immediately south of the Queen Elizabeth Way, the major expressway that links all the communities encircling the south-west corner of Lake Ontario. Often referred to as the Golden Horseshoe, this is Canada's prime business, and one-time chief industrial, heartland. Traffic on the QEW, as it is popularly known, is so consistently heavy that the provincial government has since built a second major highway further north to divert much of the truck traffic that consistently clogged its six lanes.

"Yes! That's him. I saw him up by the Oakville Mall and when I tried to follow him in the truck, he went under the QEW and I lost him."

John was not sure what he felt when Wally positively identified Dylan from the collection of photographs he had brought with him. There was certainly relief that Dylan was alive but also shock that he was still out in the elements after all this time. John looked at his watch. It was not fair to keep Gérald waiting but he could not leave without at least trying to find Dylan even though Wally was sure the dog must have moved on by that time.

Driving along the North Service Road that runs parallel to the highway, whistling and calling his name while vehicles flashed by on the Queen Elizabeth Way, proved to be a disheartening experience. John felt like he was looking for the proverbial needle in a haystack. At the base of one of the QEW bridges spanning the river that runs into Lake Ontario, he got out of the car and spent the next half-hour whistling and calling Dylan by name. Within the confines of the caverns of the bridge under-span his efforts were mockingly echoed back. Passers-by gave him strange looks and hurried on. Defeated, John returned to the car and kept his appointment with a sympathetic Gérald and an attentive Spartacus.

When Karen called that night from Kenora John again deliberately said nothing. The last thing he wanted to do was to raise her hopes only to dash them. Besides, she would be horrified to learn that Dylan had been outside all this time especially as the temperature that night was expected to plunge to -14 degrees Centigrade. As it turned out Karen had her own anxieties. Her flight to Thunder Bay was routine, but transferring to the small prop-engine plane that flies between there and Kenora, she recalled her extreme dread:

"I'm a seasoned flyer but I felt claustrophobic the moment I got on that plane. It was so small we had to bend double to get to our seats. As for the weather, when we finally landed on the small airstrip at Kenora you couldn't see in front of you."

She told John: "The way I feel, I don't know how I'm going to get back on that plane to come home."

John could feel her agitation over the long distance lines. It was sufficient to cover his own loss of equilibrium at what was happening on the home front.

The sharply falling temperatures nagged at him, so after a hurried supper he drove back to Oakville. Thinking Dylan was likely moving still further westward, he decided to concentrate his search at the foot of another QEW bridge, west of the large shopping mall where Dylan had last been seen scavenging around the big garbage bins. Even though John had dressed warmly in anticipation of the lowering temperatures, he could feel the chill getting to him. Once more he resumed his whistling and calling. Once more he was left feeling totally defeated. It was hopeless. What could he be thinking about? Dylan could be anywhere.

John returned home and crawled into bed. At 4:00 a.m. he woke with a start. Even though he knew it had to be his imagination he was convinced he could hear Dylan whining at the front door. As before it was the phantoms of the night but now John could not go back to sleep so he picked up a book.

He was still engrossed in Nelson Mandela's auto-biography, *A Long Walk to Freedom*, when Karen called just after 6:30 a.m. For her it was an hour earlier because of the one hour time difference. Even though she had been full of her own concerns, she had sensed that something was worrying John, that he was holding something back. Still he refrained from saying anything. Knowing that

John can be stubborn when he feels he is being pushed, Karen wisely rang off and each embarked in their separate ways on the new day.

DAY 40

John was at work when the call came from Paula at the Oakville Humane Society. He had given her his office telephone number and now Paula was calling to say that there had been another sighting, within the last two hours. She said that a woman who lived on Falgarwood and the Eighth Line in Oakville had seen a brown-and-white dog answering to Dylan's description which, thanks to the Humane Society, had been broadcast on a local radio station. The caller thought the dog was limping.

Dismissing all the disappointments and dis-illusionment of the previous day, John decided to again take up the hunt.

The people John worked with were a solid bunch of folk. Probation Officers and their support staff have to have their feet on the ground in dealing with Young Offenders. They were also used to having a supervisor always on the go. So when he dashed out, announcing that he was "again going to look for my dog" they simply rolled their eyes and got on with their work.

The previous night John had reckoned that Dylan was moving westward. Eighth Line is east of Trafalgar Road, the main highway in Oakville from which he had conducted his first search. Now, John wondered, could

Dylan be moving eastward, towards home? John started his search, therefore, driving down the Ninth Line, which is east of the Eighth Line near where Dylan had been sighted. As before, John would stop every now and then by the side of the road, get out of the car, scan the horizon, call Dylan's name and whistle.

In this manner John finally reached the North Service Road, which with its southern counterpart runs parallel to the QEW. This once again meant having to contend with the din of the traffic on the busy highway. And once again John began to feel increasingly foolish as his efforts yielded nothing; his boyish enthusiasm was squelched by adult squeamishness. The little voices in his head were exulting over his stupidity. How could he possibly expect to find his dog after all this time?

The North Service Road actually turns north where it connects with the Eighth Line. With less and less hope, John drove up Eighth Line until he reached the intersection with Falgarwood. Now which way? John elected to turn back east and about a thousand yards past the crossroads he spotted what appeared to be a ravine on the north side of the road. John pulled to the side of the road, rolled down his driver's window, whistled and called Dylan's name. Immediately, a familiar head popped up from the grass on the hillside across the road and looked in his direction.

John stared incredulously.

"It is insufficient to say that I could not believe my eyes. I could feel my jaw drop and my eyes literally strain their sockets," he recalled. "Even now as I describe these

97

feelings, I am seized with a cold chill. This just simply could not be happening".

He had day-dreamed about this possibility, time and again, trying to imagine how he would react, how he probably would burst into a flood of tears and take Dylan with much emotion into his arms.

"Now all I could do was to sit there, open-mouthed", he said.

How long they stared at each other John could not tell. Then Dylan started forward and just at that moment a car approached from the opposite direction, travelling in the lane between them. The thought instantly flashed though John's mind:

"Oh, my God he'll be killed, and just as I've found him!"

Involuntarily he flung up his arms, imploring Dylan to stay. Both dog and car stopped. Then Dylan, noting that the car was not moving, calmly ambled across the road.

In making his wild gesture to get Dylan to stay, John had thrown open his car door and now there he half-sat, watching unbelievingly, as Dylan patiently padded his way over.

"The *child* part of me was ecstatic, the *adult* was still denying the reality", John said.

When Dylan finally reached the door, John seized him by the collar and yanked him into the car. As Dylan climbed over him to his preferred spot on the back seat, John felt a passing lick on the back of his hand.

"I sat transfixed in my seat, stunned. It still didn't seem real. Was this really Dylan? Was I going to wake up and find that this was merely a capricious delusion? It was all so anticlimactic. No ringing chords and stirring background music as in a Disney animal classic."

Instead he remembered moaning: "Is this really you, Dylan?" as he tried to engage the flood of tears that he had thought were supposed to stamp such an incredible reunion. Meanwhile his eyes had to accept the evidence.

Dylan's beautiful red-and-white coat was dulled, his ears were matted with burrs, he sported wounds over one eye, appeared to have lost a chunk out of one cheek and another from his chest, and there was what looked like an open wound, probably caused by an encounter with barbed or some other kind of wire. He was woefully thin and smelled dreadfully -- but he was unmistakably Dylan.

As John repeated Dylan's name, he acknowledged with a weak wave of his tail.

It was 2:48 p.m., Wednesday, November 29, 1996 exactly 39 days, five hours and 20 minutes since Dylan had taken off from Chorley Park in Toronto.

Epilogue

John readily admits that he is a romanticist. He loves "Happy Ending" stories. Yet dry-eyed and prosaically practical, he wasted no time in employing his cell-phone to call the Oakville Humane Society to tell them they could expect a sizeable donation. He also called his office to apprise a dumbfounded staff that he had "got my dog back" and was now going straight to the veterinarian's office.

Dr. Steve Dunn's care and concern for his patients (not to mention their sometimes over-anxious owners) is always evident.   He had been the one to broadcast Dylan's disappearance on the Internet.   When John arrived at his clinic without any prior warning, Dr. Dunn immediately took in the situation and gave Dylan a thorough examination.

In addition to the obvious wounds, Dr. Dunn found one old cut on a footpad that had long since begun to heal.   He also noted that Dylan was running a slight temperature, which was to be expected given all the stress the dog had undoubtedly experienced during the past five and a half weeks.   Knowing that whereas Dylan loves to swim but hates baths, Dr. Dunn advised that despite his strong odour, John should not stress him further by attempting to bathe him.

On the scales, Dylan's weight loss was estimated to be about eight pounds.   But other than his wounds, none of which seemed to be septic, Dylan was pro-nounced to be in remarkable health considering his incredible odyssey.   Dr. Dunn's only prescription, above and beyond the love and care he knew John and Karen would liberally dispense was a two weeks dosage of antibiotic as they gradually built up his weight.

Some changes were immediately evident.   In his reunion with a clearly delighted Fiona he seemed to have grown in stature, calmly taking her attentions in stride. Later, when she persisted in rubbing up against him to get his attention, John watched in fascination as he curled his lip, advising her in no uncertain fashion to "Back off!"

Other behavioural changes that still hold to this day were evident. It is clear that Dylan hates being confined and is constantly thrusting open closed doors. As for screen windows, the number John has had to replace is now legion.

John was naturally anxious to talk to Karen in Kenora that night. When they finally made contact, he began by saying: "I think I've found your Christmas present. What would you like for Christmas?"

Karen's response: "You know what I would like for Christmas."

"What?"

"You know".

"No, I don't", John repeated annoyingly, stubbornly forcing a definitive response.

"You know. I want Dylan back.," she said.
A deliberately long pause followed.

"Well, I've found him!" John exulted.
There was a gasp, then a shriek of pure, unadulterated joy.

John Lilly, Karen's co-trainer, was in his room next door when he heard her cry out. The previous night he had been kept awake by the partying of the occupants in the room on his other side. At first he thought the party was beginning all over again, then he realised it was coming from Karen's room. Naturally alarmed, he ran next door to find out the reason for her agitation. He was relieved to find a deliriously happy Karen.

By this time she was finally convinced that she was not dreaming. This was because John had given Dylan a dog biscuit and put the receiver by his mouth so that she could hear him crunching it. To this day, Dylan distrusts the telephone and can never fathom why the familiar voice on the other end of the phone is not in the same room.

Karen relates that when she and John Lilly finally set off for supper that night in Kenora she could not help herself, repeatedly jabbing punches into the air and whooping: "Yes! Yes! We got our dog back! We got our dog back!"

The next day, starting the training session, she delightedly told the class: "Have I got a story for you!"

That night Dylan slept on the bed, smell or no smell. Sometime during the night John remembers waking to ensure that he really was there, that it had not all been some fanciful dream.

At 6:20 a.m. he and Dylan were on the school playing grounds as usual, meeting up with some of Dylan's doggy friends, their owners expressing concern as to why they had not seen them for so long. John revelled in telling Dylan's story, proud of his dog's exploits in surviving the urban jungle. But in relating the circumstances of their reunion, he still could not get over its surreal nature. Even today every time he gives the details, John shivers involuntarily in recollection.

As a way of letting people know Dylan had been found and because it was such a great "feel good" Christmas story, John contacted *The Toronto Star* and thereby ensured Dylan's celebrity status. Under a large colour picture of the three of them, the headline proclaimed: "Dog beats odds in 36 (sic) day odyssey". The response to *The Toronto Star* story was immediate. This was how John learned about Harry Birkman's unfruitful attempts to capture Dylan the first day he took off, about George Kloet's sighting, and Kathy Barnett's finding of his name tag.

Dylan was also invited to attend a Grade 4 Current Affairs class at Falgarwood Public School, Oakville, just down the road from the ravine where John found him. It was here that one little girl made an especially perceptive comment. John had told them that Karen had declared that they would never again leave Dylan.

"What are you going to do if your wife won't go away on vacation again because of Dylan?" she asked. John laughed.

"We're still going to go away," he said.

Then, recalling the characters in his children's books who always seemed to have their dogs take part in all their adventures no matter where they went, he smiled and confessed, "You can be sure of one thing. We're going to take him with us!"

And indeed that summer, his wounds healed and scars faded, Dylan went to Newfoundland with them, enduring the 14-hour ferry between St. John's and North Sydney, Nova Scotia.

But that's another story!

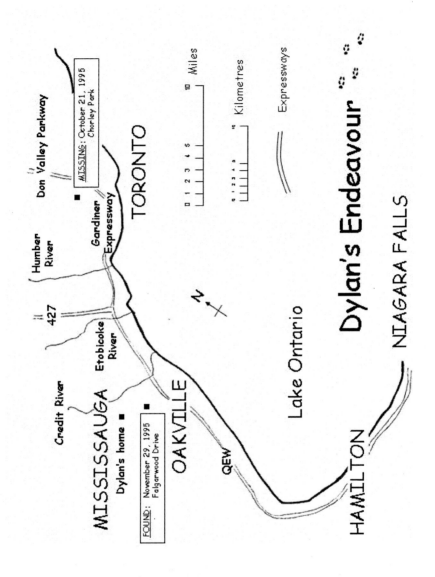

Dylan's Endeavour

MISSING: October 21, 1995
Chorley Park

Don Valley Parkway

Humber River

Gardiner Expressway

TORONTO

427

Etobicoke River

Credit River

MISSISSAUGA

Dylan's home ■

FOUND: November 29, 1995
Falgarwood Drive

OAKVILLE

QEW

Lake Ontario

HAMILTON

NIAGARA FALLS

N

Miles
10   5   0   5   10

Kilometres
0 1 2 3 4 5   5   0   5

Expressways

ISBN 155369758-8